Jewelry and Sculpture through Unit Construction

Patricia Meyerowitz

Line drawings by Jacob Meyerowitz

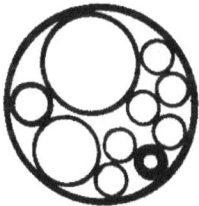

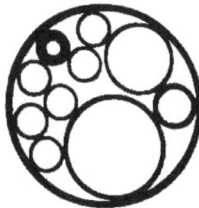

ISBN: 978-0-9931127-1-3
First published in 1967 by Studio Vista Ltd
This edition published October 2015 by Jonti Marks & Createspace
© M. Austen, J.Marks, S.Marks

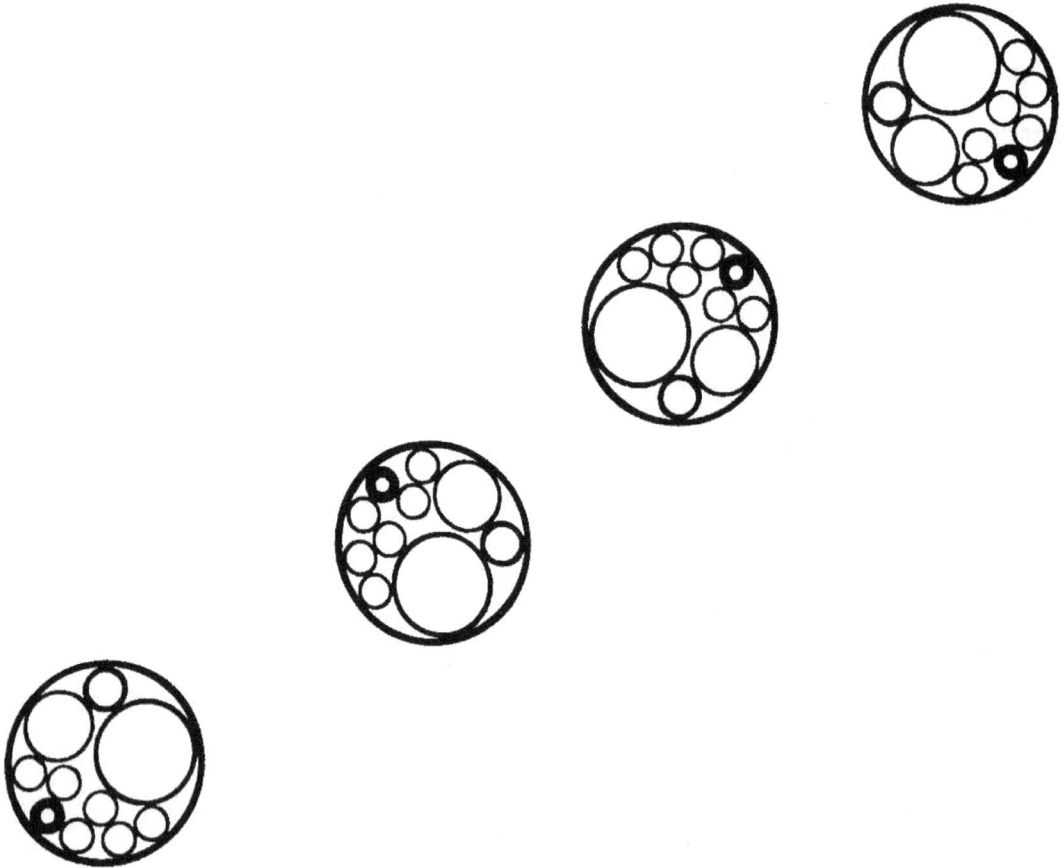

Cover photograph: Kenneth Lam - lam.kenneth@outlook.com

Patricia Meyerowitz died in 2012. At that time her book, in its second incarnation, published by Dover Publications, had been out of print for many years. Second-hand copies were available from sites like Amazon at prices ranging from the outrageously cheap to the outrageously expensive.

This new edition is essentially a reprinting of the original work and, although the format has changed slightly, the content remains exactly as it was. This means that the book, while still an invaluable, generous and relevant resource for jewellery makers and anyone interested in the principles of 'unit construction', contains aspects that are somewhat dated.

Patricia very clearly outlines the range of tools required and their uses. Since she wrote the book, however - and especially with the advent of small 'Dremel'-like tools - some of what she says is perhaps obsolete. Likewise, she uses Imperial measurements in all her descriptions and explanations of the work and this has been left unchanged. For those who are completely baffled by this system, Patricia's original conversion charts are included at the back of the book.

All of her original appendices remain intact, including the bibliography and the list of suppliers. Some of these may still exist today but, either way, the list remains as an historical record if nothing else.

Patricia's spelling is worth a comment. Even though she wrote the book before she emigrated to the States, she clearly had it in mind that her main readership would be on that side of the Atlantic. She uses the American spelling, 'jewelry' throughout the book, including in the original title, but tends to stick to English spellings of other words: 'centre' for example, or 'colour.' Once again, these idiosyncrasies have been left as they were.

Despite its age, the techniques and craftsmanship described in the book are timeless and the pieces of jewellery illustrated here and available to view in such places as the V & A Museum in London and the Hirshhorn collection in the United States are as interesting, original and beautiful now as when Patricia made them.

JAM
October 2015.

'Is jewellery art or isn't it? Is jewellery functional or isn't it? …. Art, that is real creative art, is like original research. It has no function. Art has nothing to do with what anyone wants you to do or wants it to be. Nothing to do with selling it and nothing to do with anything except you and itself. …. And so art is a process or exploration for the artist and not a description of what is already known'

Patricia Meyerowitz, lecture at Rhode Island School of Design, 1972

Patricia Meyerowitz was born in London in 1933. After marriage to Jacob Meyerowitz, architect and artist in 1957, Patricia enrolled on a course at the Central School of Arts and Crafts, London (now Central St. Martins, University of the Arts) from 1959-1960.

It was here in the late 50s that she came across the works of some of the leading jewellery designers in Britain at that time; people such as William Johnson, Head of the Central School and a leading proponent of the new ideas coming out of Europe. He brought a new energy to the school, recruiting artists and jewellery designers such as Victor Passmore, Mary Kessel, Patrick Heron, Eduardo Paolozzi and Richard Hamilton. These new recruits introduced a more improvisational technique to jewellery design. Patricia and her contemporaries, Helga Zahn, Emanual Raft, Peter Hauffe and Breon O'Casey became pioneers in jewellery design in the UK.

Patricia's deployment of Constructivist principles dominated both her jewellery and sculpture throughout her life. In 1967 Patricia published 'Making Jewellery and Sculpture through Unit Construction' – it is a step by step manual of how to make her jewellery and it remains a comprehensive text for jewellers. The book explains her principles of jewellery as pieces of art: that it can be worn or not and that the piece, as an intrinsic piece of art, is its only reason for being.

Patricia has had many exhibitions of her work, most notably at the Victoria and Albert Museum, London in 1984.

Patricia and Jacob emigrated to the United States in 1969 where she did the majority of her work, continuing to exhibit and lecture until her death in 2012.

MJA
October 2015

Contents

Introduction

Jewelry making is an enormous subject and includes many highly specialized activities such as stone-setting, enamelling, casting and engraving, each in themselves a complete study. This book is concerned with a specific approach to the making of jewelry, and therefore excludes any discussion of many of the activities usually associated with it. Nevertheless, the book opens up an enormous range of possibilities within the concept of unit construction both in jewelry and sculpture.

It is hoped that the following demonstrations and discussions will be stimulating, and that many readers will want to begin or to continue exploring the seemingly endless possibilities inherent in constructing with units of material.

Note: All tools and processes mentioned in chapters 3-7 are described in chapter 2. This chapter can be used as a practical reference, as it relates directly to what is discussed and demonstrated in the rest of the book.

1 · A creative method

This book is mainly concerned with the process of assembling small scale parts into finished objects which can be worn. The method of contemplating what these parts should be - their proportions and their relationships to each other - need not differ from that applied to sculpture, painting or any other art, and what I would term creative jewelry, like these arts, has no function. The fact that the finished piece can be worn need not determine what form it should take nor what the component parts should be, for this kind of jewelry is rewarding to make and to look at whether it is finally worn or not. One can, in fact, make a piece for its own sake with the intrinsic idea as its only reason for being.

This kind of approach has, of course, nothing to do with the designing of jewelry for mass repetition and distribution. Each finished object, like a painting, is an individual work, an original. And as a corollary to this, there is no separation between designing and making. Both are done by the same person and at the same time. The whole process is a continuous creative activity. Furthermore, since the objects are not being made solely with the intention that they should be worn, it follows that one is not bound by the dictates of fashion. Neither is it necessary to think in terms of 'fitting' jewelry such as rings, moulded bracelets and necklaces, or of surface decoration as an end in itself, or of any kind of stone setting.

In stripping away these limitations which have come to us from the past, we are left with few concepts and so have to begin thinking again about what jewelry could be. If creative jewelry is the process of assembling small scale parts into finished objects which can be worn, then how do we begin to consider what these parts can be, and how do we avoid slipping back into the trap of accepting past conventions?

Assuming the desire for choice in the work one does, one must then evolve some method of working which will constantly create alternative possibilities, for without them there is no choice. Anyone can evolve a method of working, whatever his work is, and the method I have chosen is based on control of both the materials and the various systems employed. I want to control them as much as possible so that I can understand what I am doing. If I can understand what I am doing, then I can learn from it and take the next step. If I cannot learn from what I am doing, there is no use in doing it.

Now in order to control what I do, I have to impose limitations every time I do something, and one way of arriving at this is to use repeated units of material. What I can do with them and how I choose them is determined by their attributes or qualities, which can be studied. For example, I take identical round hollow sections and think about arranging them.

Because there are so many ways of doing this, I invent a rule for myself (impose limitations) in order to begin somewhere. The sections can be placed together on a square grid or on a 60° angle grid or in some other chosen system. By deliberately limiting oneself each time, the synthesis can more easily be studied and decisions made about what the next step shall be. One begins with simple units because at first one cannot control sufficiently the multiple qualities of complex units nor the complexities of combining simple but different units. The consideration of what a simple unit is becomes the most important and perhaps the most difficult question.

It is well worth examining the work of the artists of this century who have been involved with construction as a method of art work. Their philosophies and personal approaches may differ in detail, but they have one thing in common: they have all used the constructive process. Suggestions for what to look at in their work are given at the end of this book.

It can be seen from some of their work that the concept of repetitive unit construction is not new, but my own decision to work almost exclusively in this way has led to a discovery of new sources of materials and ready-made units, and it is these materials and their use which I shall describe throughout this book. It will include not only flat sheet work and bas-relief, but also some three-dimensional possibilities of unit construction; that is to say, unit construction as sculpture.

It is not easy to say at what point jewelry becomes sculpture. It may depend upon how the work evolves. If the applied system, whatever it may be, produces a flat cut-out or a bas-relief which can easily be mounted on a chain and worn, one will limit its size with this in mind. If, however, the evolving of the system produces a totally three-dimensional construction, it can be readily displayed by mounting it on a base.

Approached from jewelry then, and within the context of the stated method, a constructive sculpture may be defined as a non-functional, three-dimensionally constructed object which is not intended to be worn. That is to say, the invented system for constructing is complete within itself and will not include any additional functional pieces which would break the system. (It should be noted that although in the following pages the practical details concerning technique apply mainly to silver and copper, the principle of unit construction applies to any material - wood, Perspex (Plexiglas), aluminium, stainless steel etc. and to any scale.)

The knowledge, then, of what a simple unit is and what one begins with may emerge through the demonstration of what can be done with repeated and combined units of material. Finally, each artist must choose a way for himself, and if it is a way which leads him, as Paul Klee put it, 'nearer to the heart of creation', then it may serve as an example to someone else.

2 · Tools and processes

Acid

The acid used for removing oxides from silver, carat golds, copper and brass is sulphuric acid. For workshop purposes, a 7-10 per cent solution is strong enough. One can either have a percentage solution made up at a chemist or dilute a concentrated solution oneself. If it is diluted in the workshop, take a Pyrex measuring jug and measure out seven or ten parts of water and pour into a glass, Pyrex or copper dish. Then pour one part of concentrated sulphuric acid into a jug and add it to the water, stirring with a glass rod. Never pour the water into the concentrated sulphuric acid. The reaction is violent, producing a great chemical heat which can be very dangerous. The reaction of the acid is more effective if either the acid or the work to be cleaned is hot. The easiest way is carefully to drop the work into the acid after soldering. Let it cool for a few moments before dropping in (see QUENCHING). A less effective or slower way is gently to heat the acid with the work immersed. In this case, use a copper or Pyrex dish.

Annealing

Metals become hardened when compressed and bent. At a certain point they crack and will not take any more hardening. The purpose of annealing is to soften the metal and make further work possible by removing the effects of this previous 'cold' working. If the metal is heated to a certain temperature, the stresses induced by working or hammering are released. At this temperature the deformed grains recrystallize into undistorted grains, restoring the soft and ductile structure to the metal.
Standard silver should not be heated above 650°C for annealing. The colour of the silver goes a dull red, and the flame should be moved across the whole surface of the metal so that every part has gone through this dull red stage. Too high a temperature or heating to a bright red colour will damage the surface of the metal. Carat golds are also annealed in the same way. 18 carat red and yellow gold anneals at 650°C and also goes a dull red.

Bench vice

A good sized bench vice is a no. 1 or 3" jaw size. The vice should be fixed to another bench or strong table. Unless the workbench itself is very much longer than the usual 3 feet, the vice will get in the way if it is fixed to it.

Binding wire

This wire is usually a fine gauge annealed iron wire used to bind pieces of metal together for soldering. When used with silver, it must always be removed before immersing work in acid (see TWEEZERS). If stronger wire is required, two lengths can be twisted together. This is the method:

Take a 2" length of heavy gauge copper wire and make a hook with a pair of round nosed pliers. Fix the straight end of this hook into the chuck of a hand drill. Cut a length of binding wire twice the length that is needed. Bend it in half and hook the centre over the copper hook in the hand drill. Now fix the two ends of the binding wire into the bench vice, and tighten so that the two wire ends remain firmly in position.

FIG 1

Stretch the double wire length out straight and turn the hand drill (fig 1). Do not twist too tightly or the wire will break. This can now be used as double thickness binding wire.

Incidentally, this is one of the ways of making filigree wire.

Blackening silver and copper

Potassium sulphide is used to blacken silver and copper. It can be obtained in crystal form or in a solution. When obtained in crystal form, it should be kept in an airtight tin as well as being wrapped in a plastic bag. This is because it changes its chemical structure when exposed to the atmosphere and becomes no longer effective. However carefully it is kept, it will eventually decompose and should then be thrown away. If a lump of potassium sulphide is cracked open, a hard core of deep yellowish brown crystal with an outer surface of a greenish substance can be seen. Only the hard brown crystal is the effective part.

Take a small chip of this hard brown crystal, about the size of a thumb nail, and place in an enamel dish containing about half a pint of water - the greenish outer surface does no harm although ineffectual. Heat the water almost to boiling point, when the crystal will have dissolved. The amounts need not be precise, but the liquid should not be transparent but a fairly dense brown. The metal can now be immersed. It will blacken immediately and can be removed after a few moments. Rinse well in water. Now use a very soft brush and, with soap and warm water, brush gently to remove any excess of the solution. Rinse again and dry with a paper towel.

Note: The metal must be absolutely clean and free of grease otherwise the solution will either have little or no effect or the blackened surface will soon begin to 'peel' away. If the solution is less concentrated, the colour will tend to be brown rather than a deep bluish-black. Practice will show the possible colour variation.

This liquid when heated gives off an offensive, sulphurous smell and should therefore be used near an open window or in a large, well ventilated room. The liquid potassium sulphide is available in bottles and is quite useful for painting on to small areas. This need not be heated.

Note: This is a concentrated liquid and ruins bristles. A small, shaped, soft wood stick, wrapped with cotton wool, is recommended for applying. This liquid also stains the hands and nails and creates a slight burning sensation on the skin, so it should be used with care. Always rinse work in water after using and then wash with a brush and warm soapy water. After the blackening process, it is possible to polish various parts of the work if desired.

The burnisher

The burnisher is a highly polished hard steel or agate tool which can be used to polish all metals which are softer than itself. Its sectional shape is elliptical, although the depth and width of the ellipse can vary. It is used by pressing it against a surface and-.t_ubbing backwards and forwards. Its action compresses and hardens-the metal, thus removing blemishes. Although it can be used along flat surfaces, there is always the danger of making them uneven. It is most useful when applied to edges which need smoothing and polishing. The burnisher does both these jobs in one action, although it cannot smooth down deep scratches. These would need filing and stoning first. It follows that the smoother the surface in the first place, the more easily the burnishing is accomplished.

When it is used along an edge it causes burring, since when metal is compressed in one direction it spreads out in another. This burring will form as a ridge along the edge of the flat surfaces and must be removed. This can be done by rubbing both flat surfaces across emery paper as described in chapter 3. The burnisher should be kept in a polished condition and wrapped up when not in use.

The care of tools

The majority of tools are forged or cast from steel. Steel rusts, and this rust causes damage and must therefore be removed immediately it appears. This is done by gently rubbing the rusted surfaces with the finest polishing emery paper. After this, a little vaseline (petroleum jelly) should be applied to the polished areas. If the tools need to be stacked away for any length of time, they must be carefully examined for signs of rust. This should be removed and then all the surfaces of the tool which are of exposed or uncovered steel should be coated with vaseline. The tools should then be wrapped, preferably in anti-rust paper or, if unavailable, newspaper or brown paper.

Note: If deep rust is allowed to develop, the tools may become permanently damaged and precision tools will be rendered useless.

Centre punches

The centre punch is a length of hard steel with a finely sharpened and pointed end (fig 2a). It is used for marking the spot for drilling. By making this depression, one can fix the drill bit in the exact position before drilling begins. This means that the drill bit does not slide across the surface, as it will surely do if the depression is not made. The centre punch can also be used for texturing a surface, and is used in conjunction with a hammer. The point is placed in position and the hammer is then used to hit the top of the punch and so cause it to sink into the metal. Hitting the punch too hard will cause distortion of the surface of the metal around the edges of the depression.

Automatic centre punch (fig 2b)

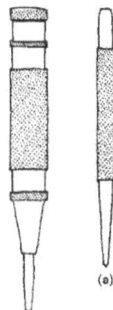

FIG 2   (b)

Except in a few instances, this very useful tool really supersedes the former centre punch because it works without the hammer. It does the same job, but the sharpened point plus a short length are fitted into a round steel barrel. This barrel has a powerful spring in it. In order to make the depression, the point is placed in position and pressed downwards. The barrel telescopes downwards until the trigger mechanism releases the spring. The spring pressure can be regulated by turning a screw at the top so that a light or heavy depression can be made.

Charcoal block

The piece of work to be soldered is usually placed either on a charcoal block or on a 'bird's nest', otherwise known as a soldering wig.

The charcoal block comes in two forms, either as pure charcoal or as a composite block. The latter is the cheaper of the two. The blocks are approximately 2j" x 4j" x 1 ", and it is a good idea to have three or four blocks available. One pure charcoal block should always be kept apart and used only for the soldering of units which need to be absolutely level with each other. Old and marked blocks can be broken up and used for supporting pieces.

Note: Never try to remove pieces of metal from the charcoal block immediately after firing when flux has been used. Allow just a moment for the flux to solidify, for in a molten state it will remove small pieces of charcoal from both types of blocks. This is bound to happen eventually, but there is no need to hasten the process. When immediate quenching is necessary, use the soldering wig where possible.

The collection of scrap

During the processes of drilling, filing and sawing of metals, a certain amount of metal wastage occurs in the form of small metal spirals when drilling and small particles of metal when filing or sawing. When working with precious metals, it is important to collect this waste material for it can be sold for refining.
Naturally the price paid for these scraps is less than the price of the metal bought in the first place, because of the cost of the refining processes. Nevertheless, it is well worth while keeping a special box or tin for the separate precious metals.

When sitting at the bench sawing or filing, place a large sheet of paper underneath the object which is being worked on. The paper will rest in the skin or on the tray, depending on which type of workbench it is, and the metal filings can then be funnelled into the scrap metal box.

When drilling, whether it is with an electric drill or alternating drill, place the wooden block into which the drilling is done on a large sheet of paper. When the metal spirals fall away, they will fall into the paper and can be put into a box in the way just described. It-is surprising how quickly this scrap material collects, even though one may not collect much during one operation.

The usual practice is to wait until a large quantity of silver has been collected before selling it for refining. This is because a set charge is made for doing this no matter how much material is delivered. For gold, the charge is little compared with the cost of the metal, so that selling an ounce of scrap gold would still be worthwhile.

Constructions and bases

If you wish to display a completed construction, you must decide on a method of doing this. The traditional method of mounting sculpture is to stand it on a base, and this way works very well with unit constructions.

The items to consider are the material of the base and the scale of it in relation to the construction. For example, the unit construction will probably be compounded of many parts and one may not therefore wish to place it on a base itself composed of several parts, for it may then compete with the construction, even appearing to be part of it. The base could consist of two or even three blocks - perhaps of diminishing sizes -but their sizes should be greater than any of the units in the construction as this will ensure their complete visual separation from it. This is one way of approaching sculpture and bases, and there may be many other ways.

Material for bases

Blocks of wood, Perspex (Plexiglas), slate, marble and ivory are all excellent materials for bases. Blocks of semi-precious stone can also be very attractive, particularly for silver and gold constructions; for example, gold on jade or silver on rose quartz. These semi-precious materials are more expensive, but having made a construction in gold one may consider it worthwhile standing it on a special base.

Methods of fixing

It has already been stated in chapter 1 that an addition for attaching anything to a construction breaks its system, and although we may accept this for jewelry, we can reject it for the pure construction. Therefore the means of fixing the construction should be part of the base. For a construction of horizontally positioned hollow sections, this attachment can take the form of a peg over which the construction fits. This peg can be fitted into the base by drilling a hole in an appropriate position and gluing it in with an epoxy resin like Araldite. The peg can be a rod of hard wood, non-ferrous metal or steel, although hard wood is preferable as it will not damage or scratch the metal of the construction. This peg should be high enough to ensure that the construction will not topple over or slide off the base when being casually handled.

Of course the detail of the peg may vary according to the nature of the construction. For example, one can glue in a short metal peg and then bend it so that it is parallel to the base, thus forming a clip. One can then slide part of one of the units between the clip and the base. Finally, the construction should not be so secured to the base that it cannot be removed, for the base would then become part of the construction. **Note:** If the unit construction is large enough, its own weight may render any fixing to a base unnecessary.

Cotter pins

Cotter pins are shaped like small hair clips (fig 3). They are made of hardened iron and have a light spring in them. They can be used to clip two flat sheets together for soldering - for example, a cutout of grid no. 1, which is to be soldered to a flat sheet, can be kept down in position by clipping on two or three cotter pins round the edges. They must be removed before dropping work into acid. Also, the heating process may anneal them and they will need to be hardened by hammering before using again. In this way, the spring can be returned to them.

FIG 3

Dividers

Dividers are instruments used to set out arcs of circles or complete circles on metal surfaces. They can also be used to step off spaces of equal length on the metal as well as for marking out parallel lines.
The spring divider is the most useful, and it is used in conjunction with the steel rule by which one measures its opening distances. This measured opening distance can then be transferred to the metal surface and appropriate markings made.

Doming block and punches (fig 4)

The doming block looks like a large dice. It is a metal cube, usually brass, with hemispherical depressions of varying sizes on all of its six sides. It comes with a set of punches which are made to fit into the depressions. It is used for making domes in metal.
For example, it is possible to take a round blank ¼" in diameter and with the use of the doming block and punches to convert it into a hemispherical shape. Place the doming block on the bench with the largest depression upwards. Place the blank in it so that it sits at the bottom (fig 5). Now take the largest punch and with an ordinary hammer or mallet hit the punch gently and then more vigorously until the blank has taken on the shape of the depression. It will be necessary to move the head of the punch all round the surface of the blank to make sure that its whole surface is touching the depression in the block. Now remove the blank and put it into the second largest depression and also use a smaller punch if necessary. Repeat the process until the required shape has been achieved. Obviously one cannot place a ½" diameter blank into the smallest of the depressions, even when the diameter of the blank has decreased as it becomes hemispherical. But a blank can be raised beyond a hemisphere, and practice will show what is possible.
Use the flat side of the chasing hammer with the smaller punches. If the dome, as it is forming, feels too hard to move any further, anneal it, although this is not usually necessary except when the original blank is very hard to begin with.

Note: These punches can also be used to make textured surfaces.

FIG 4

FIG 5

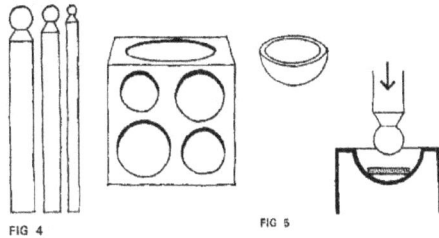

Drills and drilling

As stated in EXTRA TOOLS FOR THE WORKSHOP, an electric drill on a vertical stand is the ideal drill. However, the drill shown in fig 6 is very efficient. This drill seems to have at least three names: Archimedes drill, alternating drill, pump drill (U.S.). The drill bit is fitted into the collet and the horizontal wooden bar is wound up to the top. The drill bit is placed in the position for drilling, and then with the whole drill in a vertical position the horizontal stick is pushed downwards between the fingers. This pressure causes the string to unwind and in this way to turn the drill bit. As the string unwinds completely, pressure is removed and the string winds up again, ready for the next pushing down action.

It should be noted that this whole action causes the string to wind up in two different directions, which means that the drill bit revolves in alternate directions. There are special drill bits, called spade drills, made for this drill. They are so designed that they cut in both directions. The ordinary twist drills, however, work very well, and because the whole action of the drill is very fast, the fact that these drill bits only cut on every second turn of the drill is not very noticeable. It takes a little practice to keep the drill in a vertical position, but once this is achieved, this method of drilling is very fast. Its particular advantage over other hand drills is that the drilling can be done with one hand, leaving the other free to hold the work.

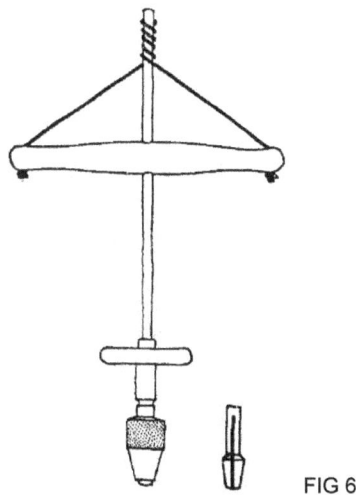

FIG 6

When drilling, place the work to be drilled on a block of wood. This will save the surface of the workbench. The block should be exchanged for another when it becomes full of holes. Also, when drilling, hold the piece to be drilled tightly in the hand, otherwise it will twist round and perhaps screw on to the drill bit.

These drills are bought with at least two different collet sizes. The collets have three jaws, and as the chuck fitting over them is tightened, so the jaws close tight on to the inserted drill bit. The smaller collet size takes the small drill bits. After a certain size, depending on the collet, it will be necessary to exchange it for the larger size to take the larger drill bits.

The hand drill is not very satisfactory for small scale work. The work has to be supported somehow, as one needs both hands to operate this drill. For larger scale work which can be held in the bench vice, it can be used more easily. It will certainly be necessary with larger diameter drill bits, as the alternating drill has its limits. The hand drill, however, is essential for easy link making (see chapter 6).

Drill bits

These drill bits come in many different sizes and are usually measured by their diameters. You may like to keep a large range of them, or if you are standardizing wire gauges, it will be possible to select the drills which make the appropriate size holes for these wires. In practice, however, it is a good idea to keep a larger selection than this.

Emery paper

Emery is a naturally occurring mixture containing between 57 per cent and 75 per cent aluminium oxide, the remainder being iron oxide impurities.

Emery paper has one surface of ground emery fixed to it by an adhesive substance. There are various grades of abrasiveness, depending on the size of the particles, but there is no need to keep a full range. Three or four grades are usually quite sufficient - the two coarsest grades, nos. 2 and 3, and the finest polishing grades, 3/0 and 4/0.

There are many ways of using emery paper, and the first thing to do is to cut the 12" x 10" sheet into manageable pieces as required. For abrading small pieces of metal such as the sides of hollow sections, take a 2" square and fold it in half. It can more easily be held in the hand and rubbed along the sides of the section. For using with a steel block which is no larger than a 5" square, cut a piece of emery paper 5" x 6". This will mean that the emery paper will overlap at opposite sides. Bend the sides down and, when rubbing a piece of metal over the surface, grip the emery over the sides of the block to prevent it sliding about. On a larger steel block, cut the emery paper to a size which will enable you to press your fingers down on the paper but will also allow enough emery surface to work on. The finest polishing emery is not very abrasive and will, like the rest, become less so with more use. This does not mean that it should be thrown away. The more the polishing emery has been used, the higher the surface polish of the metal will become, and so you should keep the used no. 4/0 as a fifth grade of polishing paper. This principle applies in a lesser degree to other grades of emery paper. They move down the abrasive grade as they become worn.

Glass paper is also very effective. It is used by carpenters and is made specially for wood. This means that metal causes the abrasive particles to wear away much more quickly, but it is very effective while it lasts. The grades to use are 11/2 for the coarse grade and then 0 and Flour for the finer grades. The finest emery paper is still the best for polishing.

Emery paper on sticks

It is possible to buy flat sticks with a covering of emery paper. They can also be made quite easily, and it will be necessary to replace the paper as it wears out.

Take a rectangular and smooth piece of wood (see page 32) and wrap a piece of emery paper round it - say 2 $^3/_4$" wide and 8" long. This will allow a wrap-over one side for joining and 4" for the handle of the stick. Fix the wrap-over with a drawing pin. You can of course fix the emery paper to any other shaped stick, and it is common practice to wrap it round needle files, simply holding it in position. Change the emery paper as necessary.

Extra tools for the workshop

An electric drill on a vertical stand is a very useful tool for repetitive work:
For example, drilling holes in several blanks which are to make a necklace is done in about half the time it takes to do it with an alternating drill.

Another power tool which has many uses is the Unimat miniature lathe. This is used for model-making and has a certain advantage in that it also converts into a vertical drill. The disadvantage is that it takes a little time to dismantle and convert into one or the other, but this is far outweighed by its general usefulness. Ideally, one would need the lathe and a drill separately.

Apart from being able to use the Unimat as a lathe, it also comes with many attachments. Because of this it is capable of performing a great variety of actions which naturally take time to learn. One of these attachments enables a circular saw to be fixed into the headstock. This is useful as a means of cutting hollow sections which are held in a small vice and fed into the saw. Solid rods cannot readily be cut in this way, although sections of round rods can be parted with a cutting tool. It is well worth investigating this power tool.

Files and filing

Files are made in different lengths, shapes and cutting surfaces. The hand files recommended have a cutting length of 6" and have a no. 1 or 2 cutting surface. The half-round and the rectangular section are two useful hand files, although other shapes may also be needed.

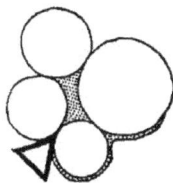
FIG 7

Needle files

These files are smaller and are therefore used over smaller areas. It is a good idea to have a set of twelve, as it will then be possible to become acquainted with many of them and in time to know which ones are the most useful. A 3" cutting length is recommended with a no. 2 cutting surface. If a set is not available, the following shapes are suggested: round, half-round, triangular and square.

Filing
Study the surface or edge to be filed and then choose a file with the shape which will most accurately fit the job. For example, if an edge as shown in fig 7 needs filing, a triangular file will allow penetration into the scalloped edges. Work to be filed can either be placed in the bench vice or, if it is small, held in the hand. In order to run the file along the area to be filed, it is necessary to hold the piece firm. This is done by pressing it against a jeweler's bench pin.
One should not be afraid of filing into this pin - that is what it is for and it can always be replaced. If the work is too small to hold in the hand, it can either be held in a pair of parallel pliers or a ring clamp. It will still be necessary to hold the work against the pin for filing.

File brush
The teeth of files can become very clogged with metal filings, and the best way of removing them is with a stiff brass hand brush. Brush across the files at the same angles as the grooves in them.

Hammers

There are many kinds of hammers with different shaped heads. Many of them are used for various kinds of forming in silver-smithing. I give here the two most frequently used for work described in this book. The hammer used for repousse and chasing is known as a repoussé or chasing hammer (fig 8a). The ball head can be used for texturing and hardening of metals and also for riveting (see chapter 4). The flat head is used in conjunction with all small punches including the repoussé and chasing punches. The larger punches can be used with any hammer that has a broad flat face.

FIG 8

Another useful hammer is the ball pein (fig 8b). The flat head of this hammer is actually very slightly curved and can be used to harden, flatten and stretch metal without too much marking or texturing of the surface.
A wooden or rawhide mallet is essential in the workshop. It is used for flattening or forming metal, but does not harden or mark it to such a degree as a steel hammer.

Hands

Our hands are our most valuable and most important tools and must be treated as such. However, a certain amount of damage to them is inevitable, even for the most skilful worker.
The most common accidents occur during hammering, needle filing and sawing. We hammer our fingers and drive files and saws into them. When the skin is broken, wash the wound immediately. If the damage is caused during sawing, let the blood flow under a running tap for a moment to make sure that no metal filings remain in the wound. Wash well with soapy water and a little disinfectant. Put on surgical tape to keep out the dirt.

Avoiding accidents

If you find that a similar accident often occurs during a certain action, it can be prevented by covering that part of the hand where the damage is anticipated. For example, during the sawing of links, the blade sometimes slips and lands on the thumb or first finger holding the coil. Put a covering of thin surgical tape there before beginning. While doing heavy repetitive work with the cutters or pliers, blisters may form. They are easily avoided by wearing an old pair of fabric-lined leather gloves.

Tripoli and rouge on the hands cause drying and hardening of the skin, which in turn cause the skin to crack. This can become very sore and debilitating. So always wear gloves while polishing, and also as often as necessary during any other activity. For handworkers, it seems important to maintain the sensitivity of the fingertips and this is easily lost if the skin becomes hardened.

Treating the hands

In spite of all reasonable precautions, the hands sometimes become hard, rough, stiff and sore. When this happens, it is well worth dropping work altogether for 24 hours or more to let the hands recover. Treat the hands overnight in the following way: have made up at a chemist a 50/50 solution of soap liniment and glycerine, and after washing and drying the hands, rub this solution well in. Wear a light pair of fabric gloves overnight, and if necessary repeat the following night. This mixture quickly softens the hands and therefore should not be used too often. It is far more effective than most handcreams and is very much cheaper.

Finally, it is as well to remember that even a small accident to the hands inhibits one's working facility to some extent, while a more serious accident often renders one incapable of any work at all for many days.

Jeweler's findings

This is the generic name given to all the various parts used for attaching the jewelry to a wearer. They include screws and clips for earrings, pin attachments for brooches, cuff-link attachments, fasteners for necklaces, etc. Also in the category of findings are manufactured settings for stones such as bezels and collets, jump rings, and machine-made chains, and one should always look through any part of a supplier's catalogue devoted to findings as there may be many items which could be useful as units.

It is possible to make or invent many of these parts, but it may sometimes be considered a waste of time, particularly when there are good and efficient findings available. For the work described in this book, ear-screws will be necessary, also bolt rings (fig 9) for fastening necklaces if preferred to the method described on page 47.

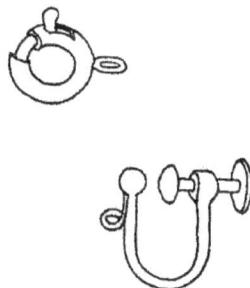

FIG 9

Joint tool

The joint tool is a form of hand vice made of hard steel, and it is used in conjunction with the saw. Its function is to hold a hollow section for cutting at right angles. The section is inserted through the triangular hole (fig 10) and the screw is then tightened, holding the hollow section in position at right angles to the tool. The saw is then used to cut away a determined length of hollow section. Do this by holding the tool handle and resting the tool on the jeweler's bench pin. Hold the frame in an almost vertical but sideways position and use the saw blade against the steel surface of the tool. With practice, it is possible to cut off an accurate right-angled section.
If preferred, the joint tool can be put in the bench vice instead of holding it in the hand.
Note: Solid rods and other shaped hollow sections can be cut in the joint tool, but it can only take small sizes.

FIG 10

Other methods of cutting rods and hollow sections (see Tube cutters)
Round hollow sections and solid rods can most easily be cut on a lathe. Most small workshops do not have such a tool, but it is often possible to find a small light engineering firm who will do this job. The cutting of other shaped hollow sections and solid rods can be more difficult, but it is still possible to have some of them cut.

The micrometer

The micrometer-screw is a device for measuring short distances accurately. The kind of micrometer which is useful in jewelry making is illustrated in fig 11 and is used for measuring the thickness of wire and sheet metal.
The rotating barrel opens and closes the gap where the material to be measured is inserted. As the spindle comes to rest on the metal, a reading is taken. There are two sets of calibrations. One is round the circumference of the barrel and measures the fractions of its rotation - these are the lesser measurements. Along the sleeve is another set of graduations which are exposed as the barrel unscrews. Each of these divisions represents one complete rotation of the barrel. To obtain the actual measure of the thickness of the material inserted into the micrometer, the readings from the two scales are added together.

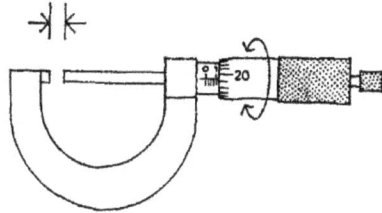

FIG 11

Paper towels

All soldering is accompanied by acid dipping and then rinsing in water. This means that work must be dried, and immediately if another soldering process is needed. Although cotton cloth is most often used, and indeed is useful to have around, the quickest and most efficient drying method is to use soft paper tissue. The best form of these tissues is that used for table napkins, as they have three or four layers. They immediately absorb all moisture and can be used over and over again until they fall apart. They also dry more quickly than cotton material.

Pliers

Pliers are among the most indispensable tools for metal workers. Their action, together with that of the tweezers, can best be described as an extension of the fingers.

Pliers are made with many nose shapes and are constructed in two different ways: there is the type constructed like a pair of scissors, that is to say, with two sides screwed or riveted to each other; and there is the type which has a box joint. The first type readily distorts under pressure, and it is really worthwhile acquiring the box joint pliers. The box joint is so designed that one side of the pliers fits through the other. This gives them greater strength and durability.

Recommended basic pliers

The common nose shapes of pliers are flat, round and half-round (fig 12). The flat and half-round pliers should have smooth jaws, that is to say, no serrations inside, as these mark the metal. The most useful length for pliers is about 5", Larger or smaller sizes may be found useful for special work.

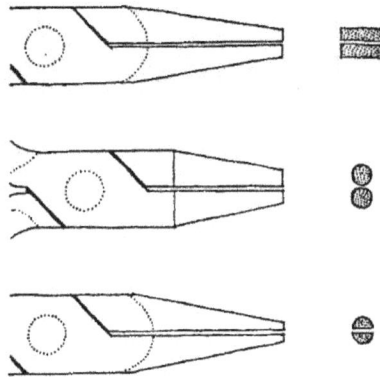

FIG 12

A pair of parallel pliers is also very useful. These pliers are so constructed that instead of opening at an angle like ordinary pliers, they open with the jaws always parallel to each other (fig 13). They are very useful for holding sheet metal and wire while filing or sawing, because the whole surface of the jaws is pressing on the held material. The parallel pliers recommended are those in which one of the jaws has a groove along it for holding wires.

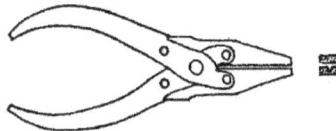

FIG 13

Polishing

Polishing is a process by which all surface defects on metals or other materials are smoothed out. Stoning out scratches with Scotch stone, the use of emery paper, tripoli and rouge are all forms of polishing, and they can each be employed at various stages of the polishing process (see under separate headings).

Machine and hand polishing
In unit construction, hand polishing is the only method recommended in most cases. Machine polishing is done at a far greater speed and it is very easy to polish away the edges of a small unit, thus totally destroying its clear articulation.

The probe

In medicine, a probe is a blunt-edged surgical instrument for exploring wounds. In soldering, it is used for moving solder around while the solder is in the state of flowing. I believe the use of a probe is essential to good soldering, and it is well worth mastering this skill.

The function of the probe is (i) to readjust small pieces of solder which move during the preliminary heating up process; and (ii), to draw or push molten solder back into a joint when it is flowing in the wrong direction.

The probe should be a thin length of hardened steel, and the most obvious thing to use is an old 4" or 6" needle file which has a point. Steel has a much higher melting temperature than non-ferrous metals, and can thus absorb more heat without melting. As solder runs to the hottest point, the object is to place the probe on the solder which has to be moved, and during the heating process to heat the probe to a slightly higher temperature. It will thus be possible to draw the solder in any direction. You can practise this process with a small sheet of copper and some silver solder.

Take a copper blank or a small flat piece of copper. Rub one surface thoroughly with fine emery paper until all signs of tarnish have disappeared. Place it on the charcoal block and flux the surface. Cut a few small pieces of silver solder and place them on the fluxed surface with a small brush which has itself been dipped into flux. Take the probe in the left hand and dip the tip of it into the flux. Begin to heat both the blank and the probe and after the flux has bubbled and melted, continue heating until the solder runs. While the solder is in a molten state try to pull, push or draw the solder around the surface with the probe. It should be possible to write with it as if it were a kind of pen. Practice will show how hot the tip of the probe needs to be.

When this is seen to work, take another blank and clean and flux the surface. Now take a short length of copper wire, and after cleaning it with emery paper lay it across the blank. Place a small piece of solder against one end of the wire on the flat surface (fig 14a).

Heat the whole piece and, after the flux has settled, take the probe and try to move the piece of solder a little way along to the right-hand side, taking care not to move the wire length. This process must be done while applying the flame and while the flux is in a molten state. If the temperature drops below the melting point of the flux, the flux will harden and the solder will just 'chip' off if moved. After this, heat more intensely until the solder flows. As it flows, use the point of the probe and draw the solder along the side until" a thin silver line can be seen from right to left (fig 14b). To keep the wire length in position, it may be necessary to scratch a line on the surface of the blank where the wire length will be positioned. Do this with a pointed punch and then use a triangular section file to deepen the line if necessary.

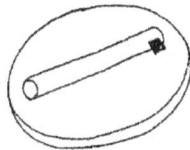
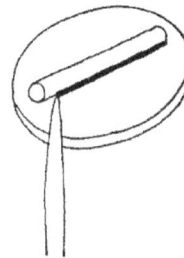

FIG 14 (a)   (b)

Note: It is very important to keep the point of the probe clean. Do this by filing off all traces of hardened flux or bits of charcoal each time before using it. Also, you should immediately acquire the habit of dipping the probe into cold water the moment it is removed from the heat. Neglecting this little action will result in an endless series of burns to the hand.

Sometimes, if the end of the probe is heated too much, the solder may transfer to it, and although it is still possible under heat to transfer it back to the joint, it may be simpler to stop the process, file off the solder and begin again. Skill in soldering develops rapidly with practice in the use of the probe, so you should never solder without having it ready in the hand.

Quenching

The method of cooling after annealing must be such as to retain the full working properties of the alloy. Some carat golds can be immediately quenched, while others need to cool to a specific temperature. Red 18 carat gold should be allowed to cool to black heat, while yellow 18 carat gold should be immediately quenched. Silver can be allowed to cool a little before quenching, and copper can immediately be quenched. The quenching when done from red heat should be in water, as quenching in acid at this heat can cause severe surface etching which may be difficult to remove.

Repoussé and chasing

Repoussé is the forming of a low or high relief on the surface of sheet metal by means of small punches. The sheet metal is set into a pitch mixture contained in a shallow wooden bowl.
The action of the punches causes the metal to expand or form into the pitch.
When the shape, say a dome, has been formed in this way, a punch with a sharper edge is used to delineate the edges of the dome (fig 15). This can be done on a steel block or on a piece of hard wood. This delineation of relief edges is known as chasing. Both these processes require a chasing or repoussé hammer.

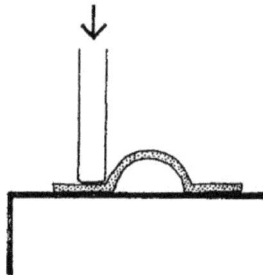

FIG 15

To set the metal into the pitch, a low flame is applied to the surface and while the pitch is in a softened state, the metal is gently pushed in without allowing the pitch to ooze over the edges. As the pitch hardens, he metal will become fixed in position. To remove the metal, it may be sufficient to turn the box over and gently tap it. If this does not work, it may be necessary to heat the pitch a little and prise the metal up.

There is another way of setting shapes in position for repousse work: Instead of using a pitch mixture, you can melt some beeswax into a small shallow tin. This mixture is very much softer than pitch and can only be used with very fine gauge metal. The results are not as smooth as they are with pitch, and there is a danger of the punch piercing the metal because of the wax giving way too easily. You should hammer very gently. Doming punches can be used for some repoussé work, although they are not the conventional punches.

The art of repoussé and chasing is a complete study in itself, and the punches used for these processes are extremely varied.

Ring clamp

The ring clamp is one of the simplest hand vices. It is shown in fig 16, and is made of hard wood. It is particularly useful for holding flat pieces which need filing, sawing or burnishing.

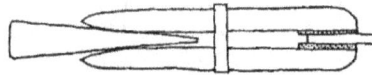

FIG 16

The work is placed between the two ends, which have patches of leather stuck to the inside to protect the work. The wedge is then inserted between the other two ends and given a sharp tap with a mallet. The brass ring keeps the two halves of the clamp together and allows the wedge to force the opposite ends tightly together, thus keeping the work firmly secured. In use, the clamp will need to be pressed against the bench pin in order to keep it steady.

Rouge

After polishing with tripoli, a final polish with rouge powder can be done in the same way. Another polishing stick should be prepared and kept specially for use with rouge. Rouge is a fine powder of iron oxide, and it should be rubbed into the leather on the polishing stick before rubbing into the metal. It can also be applied with a cloth or soft chamois leather. After using rouge, the work can be soaked in paraffin for a while to help move and dissolve any excess tripoli and rouge. Then wash well with a soft brush in warm soapy water.

Note: All polishing with rouge and tripoli should be done while wearing leather gloves (see HANDS).

Sawing

The frame
The saw frame used for the work described in this book is shown on page 66. It is also available with an adjustable frame. In theory, this means that one can insert short blade lengths, that is, broken blades, by making the distance between the two nuts shorter. In practice, however, sawing with a less than full length blade is unsatisfactory, as one really needs a full length blade for maneouvring. The adjustable saw frame is therefore unnecessary.

Blades
Blades are made in different sizes. The teeth size and distance between teeth vary. Sizes are from no. 4 down to 8/0, the latter being extremely fine. It is generally unnecessary to keep a full range of sizes. Those recommended are the finest, no. 8/0; a medium size, no. 0; and a large size, nos 3 or 4. Experience will show whether a change or an increase in the variation is necessary. Always use the finest size blade for link cutting, although a heavier wire gauge is more easily cut with a slightly larger size blade. Fine gauge material should never be cut with a coarse blade. The distance between the teeth of the blade should always be less than the thickness of the material being cut. The finer the blade, the more difficult it is to control the direction of cutting. Practice is needed.

Inserting the blade
The teeth of the blade should always be pointing downwards and away from the frame. The teeth of the finest blades cannot easily be seen, but their direction can be determined by gently rubbing the finger up and down the blade.
Insert the blade in the frame between the nuts. Make sure it is straight and then tighten one of the nuts. Before tightening the second nut, press the top part of the frame against the work bench so that the frame bends a little and the space between the nuts shortens. Tighten the second nut and release the frame. The blade is now in tension. If there is no tension, the blade will not cut properly and, furthermore, it will bend in the sawing process and snap. On the other hand, the tension should not be too great, particularly with the fine blades. The tension is always increased anyway while sawing, and if the blade is too tight to begin with, it will snap when sawing begins. Practice will show the right amount of tension needed for each blade size.
The finest blades are the most difficult to tension correctly, and one interesting way of determining this is to acquaint oneself with the pitch of sound produced when the thumb pulls lightly at the tensioned blade.

The act of sawing
The frame should always be held in a vertical position as this is the best way to achieve good and accurate sawing with this kind of frame. This means that one should be sitting in a lower position in relation to the bench than normal. The work should be about 6 to 8 inches below eye level, otherwise one cannot work with the frame in a vertical position.
The saw should not be tightly gripped, nor should too much pressure be exerted on the work as this leads to many broken blades. Sawing is an up and down action, and the process of cutting takes place during the downward movement. This, of course, relates to the teeth of the saw pointing downwards.

A little beeswax or oil will help the blade to flow more easily, but it is not recommended when cutting links which have to be soldered. This is because the wax or oil must be totally removed before soldering begins, and it is far more difficult to clean the small surface area of the link ends than it is to clean a more open surface.

Turning corners
When a sharp angular turn is necessary, the blade should be drawn up and down two or three times at the exact point of the turn. Because of the slight movement of the hand from side to side, the blade will cut a space a little bigger than its own width. This will allow the blade to turn in any direction. The blade should never be turned without first doing this, for it will surely snap.

Scotch stone - or Water-of-Ayr stone

Scotch stone is a stone which is abrasive when rubbed with water on metals. It is more abrasive than the finest grades of emery polishing paper, and has the added advantage of being able to get into difficult places as it can be sharpened to any shape with a file or a medium grade emery paper. The method of using it is to dip it in water and rub across the metal surface. As it begins to dry, use more water. A fine polishing emery paper can be used after the stoning.

The scraper

The scraper is a triangular shaped tool with three sharpened edges (fig 17). It is used, rather like a potato peeler, to remove burrs, to scrape away excess solder or to remove a thin layer of metal round an edge. Great care must be taken when using it- it cuts into the hands very easily.

FIG 17

It is also possible to use a square or lozenge shaped graver for scraping, although this may seem rather unorthodox. The graver should be cut to about 2 to 3 inches in length, then fitted into one of the special gravers' handles. This is far more comfortable to use than the scraper, and is just as effective if properly sharpened. Sharpen the left edge of the graver. This is done by rubbing it back and forth along an India stone lubricated with a light oil.

Shears or cutters

The shears are used for cutting fine gauge sheet metal and wire and solder pieces. It is not advisable to use them for cutting heavier gauge metal, as the shearing action distorts the edges of the metal. Use the saw for cutting heavier gauge metal.
The most useful shears are the scissor-like 7" long jeweler's shears.

They are made completely straight, or with the shearing part slightly curved upwards. This modification is used for cutting along curves, but for most purposes the straight shears are quite adequate.

Soldering

Apparatus
A common way of producing the heat necessary for soldering is with a French pattern blowpipe (fig 18). This consists of two pipes, one of which is for the gas supply and the second for air blown from the mouth. This means that by blowing air across the flame, you can direct and intensify the flame. The screw regulates the amount of gas flowing and therefore the size of the flame. There are several other types of soldering apparatus, including a butane gas container with a blowpipe attachment. This can be used when no other gas supply is available. There is one type which is fixed to the bench, which means there is nothing to hold in the hand so that both hands are free. The blowing is done by the same method as the French pattern blowpipe. You must decide on your own kind of apparatus, and the illustration shows the one I use. A foot bellow can be attached, eliminating the need to blow by mouth.

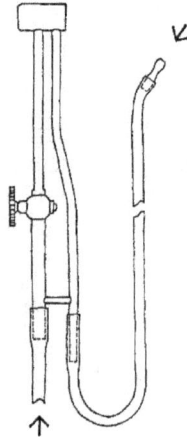

FIG 18

Preparation for soldering
The process of soldering consists in uniting two metallic surfaces by means of a fusible alloy. Silver solder is a compound of silver, copper and zinc. For British hallmarking standards, the silver content must be at least 65 per cent. It is the zinc content which regulates the melting point of the solder - the greater the zinc content, the lower the melting point.
This alloy is applied to the joining surfaces together with a flux. Flux is a substance which helps the fusing of metals by keeping the surfaces clean and preventing any kind of oxide from forming during the heating process.
With the exception of platinum and some golds, one cannot solder without flux, and it is important that it be well applied to the surfaces to be joined, as well as to the solder itself. Flux is available as borax crystals which should be ground to a thin paste with water in a flat earthenware dish; it is also available as a liquid in a bottle, and this is much the easiest form to use.

The first rule in hard soldering (easy soldering means using a lower melting point solder such as lead solder), or indeed in any kind of soldering, is to clean the surfaces to be soldered. One cannot say this too often, because when a soldering operation fails, the reason will most often be that the surfaces had a residue of grease from the fingers or tarnish was not totally removed. Never try to solder without first rubbing the surface with a fine polishing emery paper. It is always worthwhile spending an extra few moments doing this, no matter how clean the surfaces appear to be. The same is true of the solder itself. Never cut pieces of solder from a strip without first cleaning the surfaces with emery paper.

Cutting pieces of solder
To cut small pieces of solder, flatten the end of a strip of solder by putting it through a rolling mill, or flatten it with a hammer on a steel block. Now with a pair of cutters, cut into the end of the solder strip as shown in fig 19. Then cut at right angles and small pieces will fall away. The solder is cut into pieces in order to control the amount of solder applied. Obviously one can change the size of the pieces by varying the distances between the cuts. These pieces should be applied to the fluxed joints by means of a small paint brush which has been dipped into flux. The flux from the brush will now transfer itself to the pieces of solder. Always use the brush for all fluxing operations.

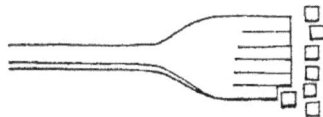

FIG 19

Grades of solder
Obviously the melting point of all solder must be below that of the material which is being soldered. Solder is available in several different melting point grades. When several soldering operations are necessary in one piece of work, it is usual to begin with a higher melting point solder so that subsequent soldering can be done with lower melting point solders. This means in theory that since each subsequent soldering operation is done with solder melting at a lower temperature than that of the previous one, there is less chance of the piece falling apart when it is repeated. However, from personal experience, I have found that a lower melting point solder is the easiest and most practical one to use, and that it is possible to make a multi-unit construction with one grade of solder. The lower melting point solder has the advantage of flowing more easily, so that with the probe you can draw it and push it around. Nevertheless, it gives strong ductile joints. This grade of solder is known as easy solder, and has a melting point of 705°-723° Centigrade. (This should not be confused with the easy solder previously mentioned; that is lead solder. The silver solder is 'easy' relative to the other silver solders.) You must decide for yourself on this question of solders, but if more than one grade is used, they should be kept separately.

Quantities
The question of how much solder is needed for a specific joint is not an easy one to answer.

There must be sufficient solder present for it to flow right through the joint so that it can just be seen at the edges. On the other hand, the solder should not be used as a kind of filler, a substitute for the material itself. It should not form large blobs at the joints, thus diminishing their clarity. Units joined together should never lose their clear articulation through bad soldering.

Note: An exercise in soldering is described under the heading of PROBE.

Moving and removing soldered units
It can sometimes happen that a piece becomes soldered in a faulty position. It is often possible, although sometimes difficult, to move or remove the unit. If it is a matter of correcting the position of a unit soldered on to a base sheet, the first thing to do is to fix the sheet in position. Do this either by pushing it against a charcoal block which itself is leaning against something heavy or immovable, or place it under the clips on the soldering wig.
Flux the badly positioned unit on the base and heat in the ordinary way. When the solder flows, push the unit gently with the probe. Do not exert too much pressure or the unit will slide way beyond the required position. Reduce the flame immediately the position of the unit has been corrected.
If this does not work, as often happens, it may be easier to remove the unit altogether. In this case, the soldering wig will be necessary and the base of the compound unit should be firmly held by the clips of the wig. Heat the piece and, when the solder flows, use a half-round pair of pliers to get hold of the unit and pull it apart from the base. It may be necessary to twist, push and pull at the unit a little in order to remove it. Be sure to flux the unit first.
Whether the unit is finally moved or removed, a residue of solder will be visible where the unit was originally placed. This can usually be removed by stoning with Scotch stone. Stone over as large an area as possible to avoid grooving. If the unit has been removed, it will now be possible to replace it with another.

Reasons for sliding units
It sometimes happens during the soldering of units that they slide quite out of position as the solder flows. The main reason for this seems to be too much solder. The unit floats in it. Another possible reason is too much blowing of air at the moment the solder is molten. This gives the floating unit a strong tail wind.

Moving and removing units in three-dimensional constructions
This is a much more dangerous and breathtaking procedure and is not at all recommended for the faint-hearted. It is all too easy to ruin an almost completed construction by trying to correct a unit which is fractionally out of position. One may need to sit for an hour or two contemplating whether it is better to continue building, leaving the slight imperfection, or whether to risk disaster by trying to correct the fault. The pursuit of perfection is itself questionable, but one should not be tempted to use this idea as a justification for producing something which is less than one's best. It is certainly something to think about. It may happen, however, that the fault is just sufficient to negate the system used in the construction, and in this case it is a matter of make or break.
Use binding wire to secure that part of the construction which will be heated during the operation. This will help to prevent other parts from sliding in all directions during the pushing or pulling.

Do not tie the binding wire too tightly. Support the construction between pieces of charcoal block and use the probe to move any unit and the pliers to remove it. If the piece to be removed is joined at several points, they must all be fluxed and evenly heated at the same moment, for unless the solder flows at each of these points at the same time, the piece will never move. One must be constantly vigilant. No over-heating must occur, and several parts of the construction will have to be watched at the same time. The colour of the silver - if silver is used - must never become brighter than a cherry red. It can be done, and the more soldering skill you develop, the more easily you will be able to perform this kind of operation.

Soldering tongs

These tongs (fig 20) are made of copper-plated mild steel and are used for holding work to be soldered. Unlike ordinary tweezers, they are so made that they come to rest in a closed position. The ends can be bent or moulded into different shapes, according to needs, with a pair of pliers.

FIG 20

The soldering wig

The soldering wig is composed of a 'nest' of iron wire arranged on a flat metal disc. Its thickness is approximately $1/2$" and its diameter 3" (fig 21). You can apply the flame to the wire and thus heat the work from underneath. The wig has a long stalk for holding in the hand while soldering. Probe users, however, will not be able to do both things at once, and it is therefore suggested that unless you are using the fixed bench type of blowpipe, where both hands are left free, this stalk should be sawn off about $3/4$" from the top. This will enable the wig to be supported between two charcoal blocks (see fig 38).

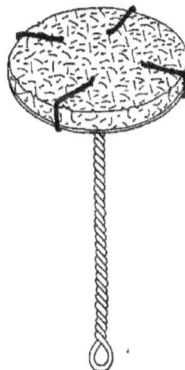

FIG 21

Steel block

The steel block is a flat block of steel with at least one flat surface machined and polished. It is an essential piece of equipment and although available in several sizes, 4" x 4" x 1" is large enough for general use. Whenever a flat, hard and smooth surface is required on which to mallet or hammer metal, the steel block will be necessary. It is also very useful when smoothing down the surfaces of blanks or the cut surfaces of hollow sections. Emery paper is placed over the flat surface of the block and the unit is rubbed across the emery as described on page 17.

Steel rule

It is important to have a good steel rule in the workshop. A 12" rule with an inch and millimetre graduation is the most useful. Apart from accurate measuring, the steel rule is used in conjunction with the dividers.

Steel square

The steel square (see fig 31) is a hard steel precision instrument for checking and establishing right angles. It is made in different sizes.

Tripoli

Tripoli is a porous granulated rock consisting mainly of decomposed siliceous matter. Jeweler's tripoli is compounded of this and a binding material such as tallow. This grease is rubbed on the metal, and the method of doing this is either on a wheel rotated by a motor or by hand with a polishing stick. None of the work in this book has been polished on a machine, and so only hand polishing will be described.

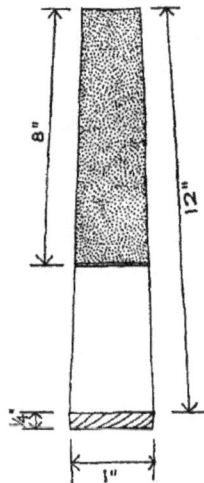

FIG 22

A strip of leather should be glued on to a strip of wood 12" x 1" x 1/4" (fig 22), and the leather strip should be the same width as the wood and 8" long. It should be stuck down with the rough side of the leather facing upwards. The tripoli can then be rubbed on to the leather, which in turn is rubbed back and forth over the metal surfaces. It should be rubbed in several directions to avoid grooving. It sometimes happens that the tripoli adheres to the metal and cannot easily be moved by the leather. Moisten the tripoli with a little paraffin (domestic kerosene) on a rag, and it should then move quite easily. Tripoli can also be applied to other than flat surfaces by using it with a cloth or a piece of leather held in the hand. The sides of round hollow sections can be polished in this way. Note All polishing with tripoli and rouge should be done while wearing leather gloves (see HANDS).

Tube cutters

There are two useful tools for cutting round hollow sections. One is simply called a tube cutter and the other a joint tool (see JOINT TOOL).

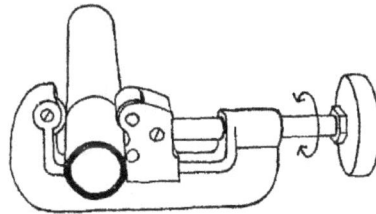

FIG 23

The tube cutter is a plumber's tool and is used for cutting copper tubing used in plumbing. There are at least three different sizes and it is shown in fig 23. On the one side is a cutting wheel, and the hollow section is placed at right angles to it. The screw is tightened until the cutting wheel is touching the section. The whole cutter is then turned by one hand, the other holding the hollow section. The cutting wheel acts like a wedge, being forced into the metal during the turning process. The screw is tightened a little more as the wheel sinks in. The cutting of a thin-walled, round, hollow section takes a few moments. The cutting process causes a burring on the inside of the section and this must be removed. It should be done as described on page 26. These cutters will cut silver and copper, but cannot be expected to cut through hollow sections with very thick walls.

Tweezers

Tweezers are used for picking up small units of material. They are also used for placing work into acid and for this action always use brass or copper tweezers.
The chrome plated or plain steel tweezers should never be in contact with silver in sulphuric acid. This is because the immersion of iron or steel into the acid causes the dissolved particles of copper present in the acid to be electro-chemically deposited on to the silver. The copper content of the acid comes from silver, silver solders and any copper which has been immersed in it.

The workbench

The traditional jeweler's workbench is constructed as in fig 24. The bench pin is a projecting peg of wood fitted to the centre of the bench, and is used to support work while filing, burnishing etc. It should be fitted so that it can be renewed when necessary. The V-shaped sawing pin, another piece of wood, enables the work to be held firmly while allowing the saw to penetrate the work through the V opening. This separate pin can be screwed on to the top surface of the bench. This allows it to be removed when not in use and also to be renewed when necessary. You can have the bench pin and the sawing pin as a single item in the centre of the workbench if you prefer.

The special height of the workbench means that for sawing and filing you can sit on a low stool and have the work just below eye level. Stooping to any kind of bench work should be avoided, as this causes all kinds of aches and pains in the neck and back. Use two or three stools of differing heights and discover which is the best height for each kind of work. An ordinary table or long bench at a height of 2' 6" is very useful for all work other than sawing, filing and soldering.

The traditional jeweler's workbench has an animal skin – usually cowhide – stretched under the round cutout of the bench. This is for catching precious metal cuttings and filings. Very fine precious metal filings tend to sink into the skin, and in order to collect them the convention is to burn the skin after several years of use. The value of this skin is usually found to have increased considerably when the precious metal filings have been collected in this way. It is much more practical, however, to use paper for collecting these filings (see COLLECTION OF SCRAP). The skin also serves the useful purpose of breaking the fall of dropped tools, thus preventing constant bending down to retrieve them from the floor. Other types of workbenches do not include this skin, but have a sliding tray about one foot under the position of the bench pin.

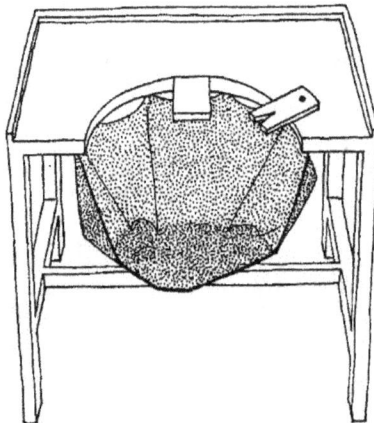

Height = 3'   FIG 24

34

An epilogue

As unit constructivists who approach the making of jewelry in an untraditional and perhaps unorthodox manner, our use of and search for tools must also follow in the same way. The tools we use should not be confined to the jewelry trade, but should be as far ranging as our explorations will take us. A plumber's tool can be just as important and useful as a precision engineering tool, and it is therefore advisable regularly to look through the journals and catalogues of the trades which might have useful tools to offer us. I say regularly, because our recognition of what is useful changes with our own personal progress.

We should remember that just as new thoughts and ideas can lead us to recognize useful tools, so new tools can lead us to extend our ideas.

3 · Hollow sections and solid rods

Hollow sections and solid rods are made in many materials from plastic to hard steel, but we are concerned with non-ferrous metals. In these metals, the hollow sections and solid rods are drawn, that is to say, they are pulled through shaped dies. They are drawn in many shapes: round, rectangular, oval, hexagonal, octagonal, fluted and so on (fig 25).

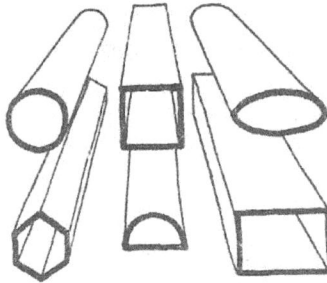

FIG 25

Hollow sections as units

In order to make a length of material into units, it must be cut into pieces (see chapter 2 - TUBE CUTTERS). For the following examples, we shall take a length of round hollow section, diameter $^5/_8$" and wall thickness $^1/_{32}$", and cut it at right angles to the length, making the sections $^1/_4$" long (fig 26). Make sure that there is no burr, that is, rough edges caused by the cutting process, on the outside or inside edges. If there is, it must be removed, as an outside burr will prevent the unit from coming into the closest contact with another unit. The burrs can be removed with a scraper, but the easiest method is to use emery paper. Place a medium grade emery paper on the steel block (fig. 27a). Taking care to keep the unit parallel with the block, rub the unit in a circular motion on the emery paper (fig 27b) until the burr almost comes away. The last thin piece can then be removed quite easily with the scraper. Turn the unit over and repeat the process on the other side. Change the grade of emery to a finer one and repeat the process.

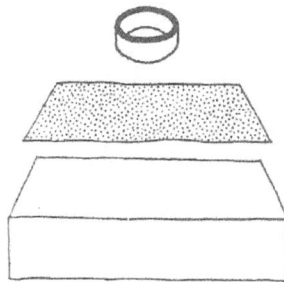

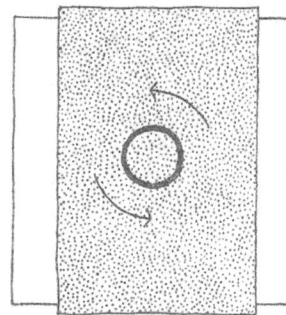

FIG 26

FIG 27   (b)

(a)

What to do with round hollow sections - Flat

The example to be described is a compound unit made up of four similar hollow sections arranged on a square grid, with one or two smaller sections added as linking devices.

Take four units as described above and arrange them on a flat surface in a square grid (fig 28). In order to solder them together in this way they must first be joined in pairs. Take a charcoal block which has a smooth and flat surface. This is essential with this kind of hollow section soldering. Take the first two units and, after making sure the sides of both are smooth and clean (use emery paper), apply flux to a section of the side of both units and place them together at this point on the charcoal block. Cut a thin strip of solder and place it alongside the joint. It is possible to place a small piece on top of the joint, but I have found the former method more successful (fig 29).

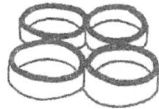

FIG 28

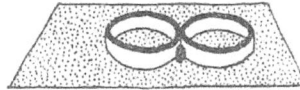

FIG 29

Begin to heat the two sections and, as the flux bubbles, make sure the units do not move. If they do, use a steel probe and, while still under heat, press the pieces together again. If they have moved apart and do not return together after the flux has melted, place another charcoal block across the top of the one in use. Place both blocks against something that will not give to pressure. One way of doing this is to fix two metal strips - copper, brass or steel - to the back edge of the workbench. It will then be possible to push the charcoal blocks up against them. The strips should be as high as two charcoal blocks placed one on top of the other. Heat the two units again and, with the steel probe, push one unit against the side of the top block and then push the other unit against it (fig 30). Make sure the solder is in the right position and also that the two units are now flat on the charcoal block. Heat until the solder runs and joins the two units together. Drop into acid after a few moments of cooling and then rinse in cold water.

Note However flat the two units may be on the charcoal block, it will always be necessary to smooth the compound unit with emery paper on the steel block, as shown in fig 27. This must be done until all signs of the joint have disappeared from both flat surfaces.

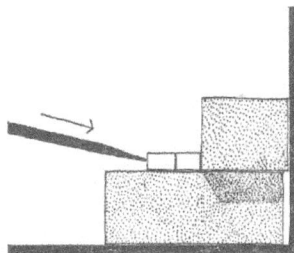

FIG 30

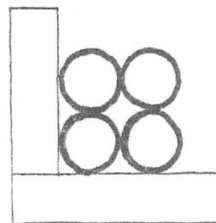

FIG 31

Repeat this process with another two units. Now to join these compound units together, take the two pairs and place them together to form a square on the charcoal block. Flux the two points of contact and, with a steel square (fig 31), make sure they really are at right angles to each other. Place solder at the two points of contact, either on the inside or outside, and begin to heat gently. Just before the solder runs, maintain the temperature while making sure the two compound units have kept their position and are flat. Use the probe if necessary. Continue heating until the solder flows, and when it is seen to flow through the joints, withdraw the flame. Great care must be taken not to overheat the joints of the compound units, and there is no reason why these first joints should come apart if the flame is carefully controlled and directed to those parts to be soldered. As before, drop the compound unit - now compounded of four units - into acid and then rinse in water. Use emery paper on the steel block again and smooth both flat surfaces until the joints can no longer be seen.

Note: It may be asked why binding wire has not been suggested for keeping these units together during soldering. The answer is that it is more difficult to bind the units as accurately as they can be when they stand naturally on a flat piece of charcoal. The slightest movement after the binding, and the soldering process will be wasted. However, some people may find this the simpler of the methods.

Polishing the compound unit
This compound unit of four units can now be polished, but before attempting to polish, make sure there is no burring on the inside or outside edges of the hollow sections. Polishing this kind of compound unit is best done with a hand polishing stick for both flat surfaces, and emery and chamois leather for the sides (see chapter 2).

What to do with the compound unit
This compound unit can be used as a necklace unit or an earring. Or, if it is made on a larger scale, it could hang as a pendant.

Methods of joining compound units of hollow sections
One way of joining these compound units to each other is to solder little 'ears' to each side, if they are to be used as necklace units, or to one side if used as earrings or pendants. The 'ears' should be made of small, round hollow sections.
In this case, the larger hollow sections are $5/8$" in diameter, and so a good size for the smaller sections would be about $3/32$". Put a length of this hollow section in a joint tool and cut off two short lengths - say, $3/32$" each. Make sure there is no burring on the inside or outside of the sections. Do this by threading each unit one at a time on to a round needle file held in the right hand. With the left hand, take a small piece of fine emery paper and bend it partly round the section on the needle file. Roll the file back and forth between the fingers, allowing the file to remove the inner burr while the emery paper removes the outer burr. Do not twist too vigorously in a clockwise direction, as the unit may 'screw' tightly on to the needle file and be difficult to remove (fig 32).

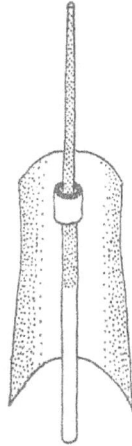

FIG 32

When both small sections are ready, take one of them and thread a short length of binding wire through it and through one of the large sections. Flux the joining position and then tighten the binding wire so that the small section remains in position (fig 33).

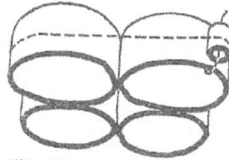

FIG 33

Do not twist the binding wire too tightly, as it will mark the edges of the larger unit. Now place a small strip of solder at the joint. There are many ways of positioning the compound unit for this additional soldering, but I have found the best method is to stand it on a charcoal block between two smaller pieces of charcoal (fig 34).

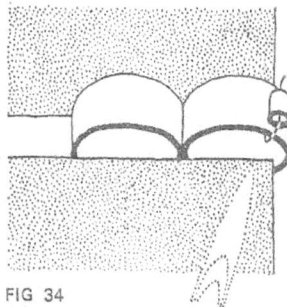

FIG 34

If care is taken to heat only the relevant area, nothing will come apart. When this is soldered, place in water to cool and then remove the binding wire. Silver and iron binding wire must not be placed in acid at the same time (see chapter 2 - TWEEZERS). Fix the other small section on the opposite side of the compound unit, and when this has been soldered in position, links may be attached to these 'ears' and the compound unit used as a necklace unit. With only one small section soldered in position, this compound unit could hang as an earring if it were made on a smaller scale, or as a pendant hanging in a diamond shape.

An alternative method of binding the small sections in position is to place the binding wire round the whole piece as shown in fig 33 (dotted line). Again, great care must be taken not to pull the wire too tight, as it can easily distort the shape of the compound unit under heat as well as biting into the silver.

Extended uses of the round hollow section
There are many ways of arranging these round hollow sections, and here are just a few including round hollow sections inside each other (fig 35) and hollow sections in combination with sections of solid rod (fig 36).

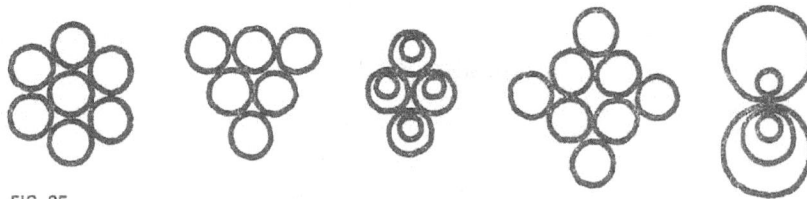

FIG 35

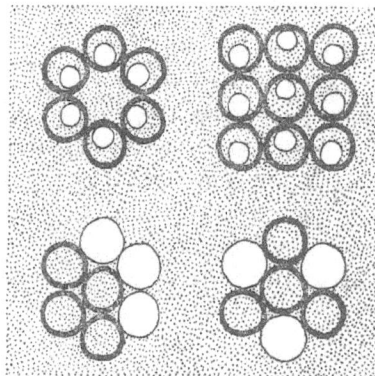

FIG 36

Hollow sections used in bas-relief (fig 37)

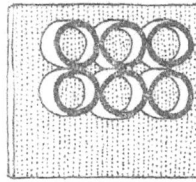 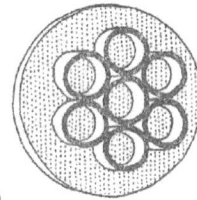

FIG 37 (a)   (b)

The total variety of hollow sections can be soldered on to flat surfaces. They can be soldered in single or compound units.

In the case of compound units, solder the units together first and then place the compound unit on a flat sheet of metal after smoothing and fluxing the surface. Cut small pieces of solder and place them either inside the hollow sections or outside, close against them on the flat surface. Place the whole piece on the soldering wig, which is supported between two charcoal blocks. It is a good idea to cut off the stalk of the soldering wig so that it can easily be placed on the blocks, for probe users will not be able to hold the soldering wig at the same time (fig 38). With the steel probe in the left hand, slightly raise one side of the metal sheet and gently apply flame under the surface. After the flux has bubbled, make sure the unit or compound unit is in the right position and that the solder has not moved. Continue to heat gently and, as the solder runs, direct the flame to the top surface.

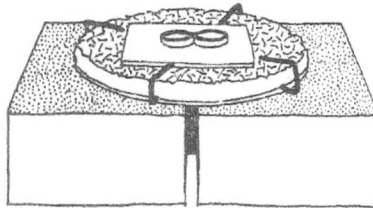

FIG 38

Note: The flat pieces on to which hollow sections can be soldered need not be cut out, unless particular shapes are needed. They can be stampings or blanks (see chapter 4).

If an overlap of the flat surface is not wanted, it can be cut away with a fine saw, the process of doing this being the same as shown in fig 65. To smooth the edges of the flat sheet so that they merge into the sides of the hollow sections, first take a triangular needle file and carefully file these edges until they do not project at all beyond the sides of the hollow sections. Now remove the file marks with a Scotch stone and then use a burnisher, taking care not to mark the sides of the hollow sections. To join this compound unit to other similar ones, for necklaces or as an earring or pendant, use the same method as shown in fig 33.

Three-dimensional building with hollow sections
Take a thin round hollow section and, after preparing it in the way already described, place it on a flat charcoal block. Take an identical piece and place it on top but slightly dislocated. Choose a definite position, for example, a quarter way across, so that it remains horizontal and does not tip over. When the position of joining has been decided, flux both the points of contact and place small pieces of solder at these points on the rim of the bottom unit (fig 39). Heat slowly from all directions, and concentrate the flame more directly as the melting point of the solder is reached. If the solder does not run easily into the joint, it should be 'drawn' into it by using the probe. If the hollow section has a thicker wall than, say, ·03" or more, it is better to place two small pieces of solder on either side of the upper hollow section. If one piece of solder is used, say on the inside, it is possible to concentrate the flame on the other side of the joint as the solder is running and draw the solder through. This will happen quite easily as long as both the top and bottom pieces are equally heated, as solder *always* runs to the hottest point.

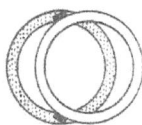

FIG 39

To continue building, take a third piece and place it in direct line above the first unit, or in some other chosen system (see chapter 1). Solder in the same way, heating the first piece for a few moments only and then concentrating on the two relevant units. There is no need to shield the previous joints, and they will not run if the flame is not directed at them and the upper units are not overheated. Place the fourth unit and solder in the same way, heating the second unit for only a few moments before concentrating on the third and fourth units. This process can be repeated as many times as necessary, and one way of knowing when to stop is to consider the question of proportion, that is, total width related to height.
 If a more complex building system is used, the system will have to evolve itself completely, or at least to some specific point of stopping. It is also important to think about the strength of joints related to weight of material.

Three-dimensional compound unit building
Instead of single units, you may wish to build with compound units, for example, two round hollow sections soldered together (fig 40a). You should proceed in the same way, the only difference being that there will now be five or six points of contact for soldering, depending on exactly how the compound units are positioned on top of each other (fig 40b).
It is absolutely essential for each compound unit - this also applies to single units - to be flat and smoothed over with fine polishing emery paper before building begins. If they are not in this condition, the whole procedure will be a waste of time, for it will then be very difficult, and probably impossible, to obtain a good join, or indeed any kind of join. After each firing and cooling, the top surface must again be smoothed with fine polishing emery paper to remove any trace of tarnish or hardened flux. Again, if care is taken, the centre joint of the compound unit will not be affected.

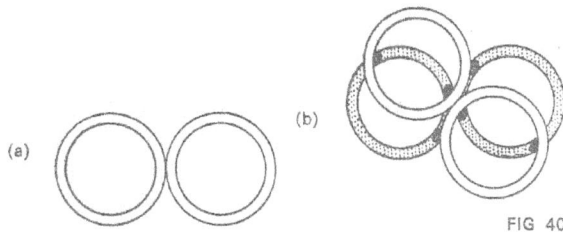

FIG 40

Cutting hollow sections at angles
Just as you can construct with hollow sections cut off at right angles, so you can use these sections cut off at other angles. This opens up even further the concept of unit construction, and if you begin to consider, for example, cutting a rectangular hollow section at an angle, you will get a further glimpse of the enormity of the whole subject. If this rectangular section is cut at such an angle that the rectangular hollow opening becomes a square, it can then be joined together in many different ways - square to square, rectangular side to rectangular side, a combination of both, and so on.
One cannot easily imagine the possibilities, and in order to study them one would have to go through the process of building them. This is, of course, true of all construction work in art: you cannot altogether decide beforehand what is to be done. You have to explore while doing it.
The actual cutting of the sections at angles presents a problem. Until you have some kind of motorized cutting machine for accurate, repeated cutting, it is not worth while tackling this particular aspect of unit construction. The small model-making lathe described in chapter 2 has the capacity for doing this job.

Note: All these processes described for flat unit construction and three-dimensional unit construction apply to all shapes of hollow sections. You should refer to the construction notes to see some possible extensions of these ideas.

Finishes for hollow section work
It is not at all easy to polish the insides of small hollow sections, and they will inevitably tarnish more quickly than surfaces which are often handled. One way of finishing these pieces is to cause them to tarnish chemically and so control the colour. Dip them into a solution of potassium sulphide (see chapter 2). After rinsing in clear water and drying, highly polish both flat surfaces with a hand polisher. In the case of bas-relief, also polish the sides of the flat surface. With a rag or piece of chamois leather, you can lightly polish parts of the sides of the hollow sections. The contrast between the blackened silver or copper and the high polish is very attractive.

Solid rods
Thin sections of round metal rods can be thought of as round blanks, but thicker sections which cannot easily be stamped from a sheet without distorting the edges too much for use can be cut on a lathe.
These sections can be dealt with in the same way as hollow sections, that is, joined together at their sides as shown in fig 36, or used for three-dimensional building as for hollow sections. Other shaped solid rods, rectangular, square and so on, can also be used in similar ways, although cutting them into units is not an easy matter. They should be cut on a fairly powerful circular or band saw.

4 · Blanks, stampings, washers and rivets

Regular flat shapes of material which have been stamped out from a sheet with a punch and die are called blanks: for example, circles, squares, rectangles and so on. Stampings are made in the same way, but can be any conceivable shape and are mostly designed to do a specific job. Sometimes more than one stamping action will be needed to make the required shape.
Washers differ from blanks only in that they have a hole in the middle.
They are mostly circular, but occasionally one comes across square washers. They are mainly used in conjunction with nuts and bolts, and are made to standard sizes in brass and copper, although it is often possible to obtain other sizes.
Rivets are fasteners, and are used to connect together permanently two or more sheets of metal. They are also made to standard sizes. The length and diameter of the shank and shape of the head can vary considerably. The head can be flat, round or domed, and the flat-headed rivets can also be countersunk.

Blanks

These shapes include the burrs which come from perforated sheets (see chapter 5). Round blanks in all metals can be used in endless ways.

Simple necklaces
First, here is a description of a necklace made with round blanks and using a simple clasp.
Take silver or copper blanks 1" in diameter. With a centre punch and chasing hammer - or automatic centre punch - make indentations and then drill two holes. Fourteen to sixteen blanks will be needed to make a necklace.

Note: The position of the holes determines how the units will hang. The holes can be placed on a determined grid, and an obvious one is on the two points of an equilateral triangle (fig 41).

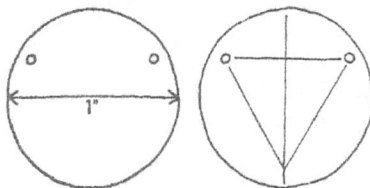

FIG 41

When all the holes are drilled, the burring round the holes caused by drilling must be removed. Place a piece of medium grade emery paper on a steel block and put the first blank flat on it. With the first or second finger, press down in the middle of the blank and move it across the emery paper in a circular motion. Reverse the blank and repeat the process. Change the emery paper for a very fine polishing grade, and this will give a fine matt finish to both surfaces. If the finger slips on the blank, moisten it very slightly with water or wear a rubber finger stall. If a high polish is required, use the polishing stick after the fine emery paper.

The edge of the blank should also be polished, and this can be done by holding the blank between the thumb and first finger of one hand and rubbing a small piece of fine emery paper to and fro across the edges with the other hand. Revolve the blank until the whole edge is polished. Use two grades of emery paper if necessary, and finish it with chamois leather and rouge.

When all the blanks are prepared, you must think about joining them.

If they are placed together in a line, it can be seen that the space between the holes of each separate blank is too great a distance to join them with one small, fine link. One has to think a great deal about link sizes and diameters related to wire gauges, as you cannot use a large diameter link unless you use a heavy gauge wire. The reason is a matter of strength and also of scale and proportion. One also has to think about the size of the link compared with the main unit of the necklace; whether this main unit, in this case a 1" diameter blank, is a heavy or fine gauge. The joining link should never be more powerful than the main unit, as then the link *becomes* the main unit.

Assuming our main unit, the blank, is a fine gauge ·018", then a fine gauge wire will be needed. In this case the link must not be too wide in diameter. This in turn means that it will be too small to stretch the distance between the main units. An intermediate link will therefore be needed (fig 42).

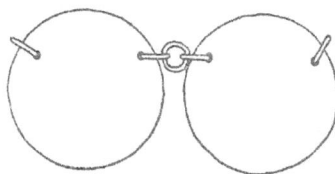

FIG 42

Now you have to decide what size the intermediate link should be. The first consideration is: shall the joining links be simply a short length of chain between each unit? If so, the links should all be the same size. The second consideration is: do you wish to introduce a secondary unit into the necklace? If so, it is possible to make the centre link from a heavier gauge wire and make its diameter greater than the links attached to the main unit. For the purpose of this example, let us assume that the units will be joined by a short chain length. If the circle unit is 1" in diameter, and gauge ·018", the links can be made with ·028" wire made on rod no. 4 (see chapter 6). After these links have been made, take one blank and with two pairs of pliers - flat or half round - thread one link through one of the holes, flux the joint and then close the link.

Take the soldering tongs and hold the blank with them so that the first link to be soldered hangs downward with the joint at the bottom. Rest the tongs on a charcoal block (fig 43), and after placing a small piece of solder on the joint, lift the link slightly upwards with the probe.

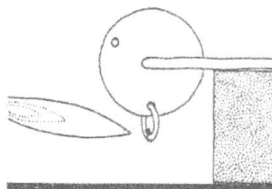

FIG 43

Now concentrate the flame on the joint. The solder should run and flow through the joint but, if this does not happen immediately, move the link up and down a little, keeping the flame at the joint. The probe should be held to the side of the joint, although if the solder does not run, it may help to hold it directly under the joint. The probe is then heated, together with the silver, and as it absorbs more heat, the solder should run through the joint towards it. Drop the blank into acid after a few moments, rinse in water and dry on a paper towel. Thread the second link through the second hole and solder that. Do the same thing with the remaining blanks.

Note: Care must be taken in this process as the probe can easily become soldered to the joint. If this happens the solder will have to be run again after fluxing the joint and the probe pulled away while the solder is flowing. Any solder on the probe must be filed off.

Joining the units
Take a small link with the pliers and thread it through the links of two separate blanks as shown in fig 42. Flux the joint and close the link. Hold the two blanks together in the tongs so that the centre link hangs down with the joint at the bottom as previously shown. Rest the tongs on the charcoal block as before and, after placing a small piece of solder on the joint, heat until the solder runs. Place the units, or just the soldered joint, in acid, rinse in water and dry. Join the next pair of units together and, when they are all in groups of four, join these groups together until all the blanks are together in one line.

Clasp making
Clasp making can be a complete study in itself, but I give here only the method I use most frequently (fig 44).

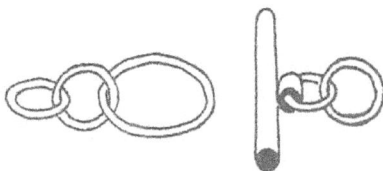

FIG 44

Take a straight length of wire ·062" and cut off a ³/₄" length. Do this by using the joint tool, as cutting wire of this thickness with the cutters will distort the end faces of the wire. Now take a length of round hollow section approximately ·094" in diameter and with the joint tool cut a length ·062". Smooth both ends of the section and then thread it on to a needle file for cleaning the side surfaces. Take the wire length and smooth both flat ends and side surface. Now place this length of wire on a flat charcoal block and put the hollow section half-way along its side. Flux the point of contact and place a piece of solder there (fig 45).

FIG 45

Heat slowly and, after the flux has bubbled, adjust the position of the hollow section with the probe. Continue to heat until the solder flows. Place in acid, rinse in water and then dry. Now take a small link, the same size as the necklace links, and thread it through the hollow section. Flux the joint and close the unit. Lay the whole piece on the charcoal block as before, so that the link joint is furthest away from the hollow section and resting on the charcoal block. Lay a piece of solder on top of the joint and, with the probe, lift the link slightly. Heat gently until the solder flows. Join one more link to this link. In order to do this, it may be easier to hold the wire length in the soldering tongs so that the new link hangs down for soldering. This piece should now be joined to one end of the necklace. The blanks at either end will already have a link in them. Take another link and thread it through the loose link on the clasp piece and the link on the blank. Flux the joint and close. Solder by holding the piece in the tongs or by laying on the charcoal block, whichever is the easier. Always have the probe ready to loosen the link and to help the solder flow.

On the other end of the necklace, attach a larger, heavier wire gauge link through which to thread the wire bar in order to fasten the necklace. To do this, take a length of wire ·036" and make links on rod no. 6. Take one of them and thread through the link on the last blank of the necklace; flux the joint and close the link. Lay the relevant part of the necklace on the charcoal block and solder the heavy link. Keep the large links in a special place, as they will be needed again some time. This completes the clasp (fig 46) and the necklace.

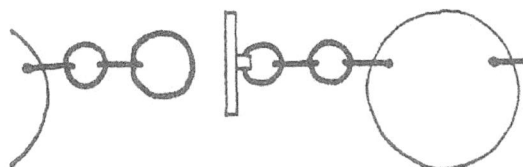

FIG 46

Alternative method

In place of the wire bar, you can use a length of rectangular wire. Drill a hole in the middle and then thread the link through this hole.

To make sure it is strong enough, it should be at least $1/32$" thick and $1/8$" wide (fig 47).

Note: It is important not to make the clasp ring too large, or the bar of the clasp will come apart as easily as it fits together. It should, however, be large enough for the bar and the links to pass through.

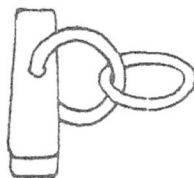

FIG 47

Possible variations of this simple necklace
1 Use another unit between the circular blanks (fig 48).
2 Solder units on to the blanks. For example, smaller blanks or hollow sections as in chapter 3.
3 Shape the blanks in the doming block before joining them to each other.
4 Texture blanks with chasing hammer. This process also hardens the metal and may in fact be necessary if the blanks are very thin. It should be done as a last process before attaching the links. Take care not to distort the holes with hammering. If this happens, take a round needle file and twist it gently through the hole until it becomes circular again.

FIG 48

Necklace making without soldering
For beginners who cannot yet solder, it is possible to make the first or second necklace. Simply make it on a slightly heavier scale. Take round copper blanks ·032" and heavier gauge wire ·048". This means that the links will be relatively stronger and can just be closed without soldering. Use the second variation of the clasp. There are endless varieties and extensions of these simple unit necklaces, as the main unit could be any shape. Always think about shape relationships when choosing primary and secondary units.

Note: It is not my practice to leave open links of precious metal - silver or gold - and I therefore advise beginners to use copper or brass until they learn to solder.

Washers

Washers can be used as primary or secondary units in a necklace. It may not be necessary to drill any holes for the joining links if they are large enough to thread through the centre hole of the washer. Some of the larger washers will need extra holes, as the links needed to thread through the centre hole would be much too large for necklace making. The washer can be used as the primary or secondary unit in conjunction with the round blank.

Irregular shaped stampings - electrical contacts
Although these stampings are made in different metals, we are here concerned with silver. The stampings now referred to are known as 'electrical contacts' and are stamped out in pure silver. They are used in the electronics and electrical industries, and these special pieces are designed for use in many kinds of apparatus where electricity, and therefore electrical circuits, are fundamental to the apparatus. Pure silver is a very good conductor of electricity, and in fact has the highest conductivity of all metals.

There are many technical reasons why pure silver cannot always be used as contact material. For example, although pure silver does not oxidize, it easily forms a tarnish film of silver sulphide. This film will cause a break in the electrical current if allowed to develop. On the other hand, if the switching mechanism in the electrical apparatus operates with a wiping action, this will constantly clean the surface of the silver and therefore no tarnishing occurs. If, however, contact occurs simply by the two silver pieces coming together, the tarnish film may form, and therefore in this instance silver will not be the correct metal to use. A combination of gold and silver or palladium and silver may be used instead. Also, mechanical wear has to be taken into consideration.

Pure silver is soft and, in certain circumstances, constant rubbing will cause rapid wearing away of the metal. This will mean a harder metal is required, or an alloy of silver and another metal to harden the silver. These details, however, although interesting, are electrical and chemical engineering problems and do not concern us here.

For our purposes, these silver electrical contacts are ready-made units which can be used to make necklaces, pendants, earrings and so on. Although certain electrical contacts, such as silver rivets, are standard units, no list of other available units can be given because the range is constantly changing according to industrial needs.

How to approach irregular shapes
When you are confronted with any kind of complex shape, in order to understand it you must analyse it. That is to say, you must study its angles, curves, different shaped surfaces and so on. You are interested in its qualities or properties, for you have to take them into consideration in order to decide what you can do with the unit. For example, if you have a flat shape like fig 49, you can say that it is a rectangle with one square 'foot' protruding from one of its lengths.

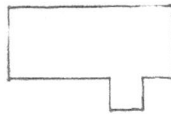

FIG 49

You can measure and list many things about this unit: its gauge, length, width, the point along the side at which the 'foot' protrudes. There is no point in taking the easy way out: that is, cutting off the foot to make it a regular rectangle. It has come with this 'foot' and you must try to use it. You may simply make a necklace as shown in fig 50a, or a variation (fig 50b), or you can modify its shape by cutting out with a saw an identical area in a number of positions (fig 51).

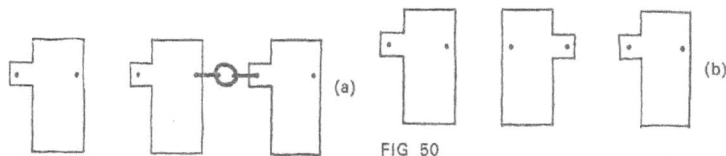

FIG 50

If this latter operation is decided on, cut out the pieces carefully with a fine saw, for they may also be used at some other time. There are many other possible modifications, but they should always be related to the original shape. The point is that these irregular stampings can lead to many new discoveries about shapes which you might never have made if you had not had such irregular shapes in the first place. You can, of course, invent a multitude of irregular shapes and cut them out, but there is no reason to invent one rather than another and so where could one begin. These ready-made pieces help one to begin thinking about irregular shapes. They come as industrial pieces designed to do a specific job, but we have more freedom than industry, and can do with them anything we can invent through study and practice.

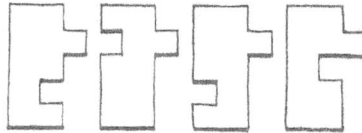

FIG 51

Rivets (fig 52)

Silver rivets are principally used as electrical contacts. They are used to rivet together the flat stampings where hard soldering cannot be employed for technical reasons. Copper rivets are also used in the electrical industries and in the sheet metal industries.
For our purposes flat-headed rivets have an advantage over the round or dome heads in that they can be soldered on to flat surfaces at either end as well as being used in their functional capacity.

FIG 52

Soldering with flat-headed rivets
Take a round silver blank $3/4$" in diameter and a small flat-headed silver rivet. Think about positioning it head down on the surface.
There are two basic possibilities when thinking about this kind of problem: either you just use an arbitrary position, or you invent a system for placing it. This book is concerned with system and order and so naturally I choose this way. The simplest method of studying the possibilities is by drawing. Draw a circle on paper and construct two right-angled axes as shown in fig 53a.

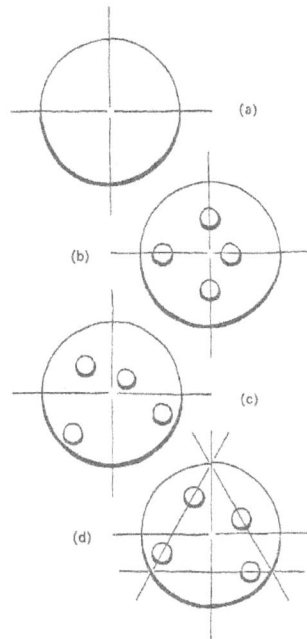

FIG 53

You now have a grid on or around which you could place one or more rivets. You can position them along the axes as shown in fig 53b, or you can use the areas within the quadrants as in fig 53c. You could also develop a more complex grid and use it in a similar way for positioning the rivet or, indeed, any added unit (fig 53d). When making a necklace with these units, that is to say, with a blank and something soldered to it, as the first step one should try to decide the position of the unit or units to be attached. The reason is that the holes for joining the units should be drilled before any soldering is attempted, so that the surface of the blank can easily be smoothed and the holes deburred in the usual way. If something is already attached to the surface, it will be more difficult to achieve the same kind of overall smoothness.

Attaching the rivet to the blank
Having decided on the position of the unit or units to be attached, make marks with the centre punch for drilling the holes. After the holes have been drilled, smooth and polish the surface.
Now take the rivet and, holding its shank between thumb and first finger, smooth the head with the finest polishing emery paper on the steel block. Then place the blank on the soldering wig and flux the position of soldering. Place the rivet head down in its correct position. Cut a small piece of solder and place it on the blank at the side of the rivet-head (fig 54).

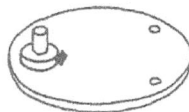

FIG 54

Direct flame gently under the blank, lifting it very carefully with the probe if necessary. The flame must be very gently applied until the flux has bubbled. Check the position of the rivet and solder, and then apply heat more vigorously until the solder flows. The flame can be directed to the top surface as the solder runs, but it should not be too high as the force of too much air in the flame can blow the rivet out of position and sometimes these added units can slide on the flowing solder. This may also mean that too much solder has been used. This rivet can also be soldered to the blank surface with the shank downwards. Obviously this will be a more difficult soldering operation, as the flat end surface of the shank is very much smaller than the head surface. When smoothing this end surface, great care must be taken not to distort it by too much rubbing on the emery paper, otherwise it will no longer stand in a vertical position for soldering and will topple over. Solder it in the same way as described before, but do not lift the blank with the probe or the rivet will surely topple over. Direct a small pointing flame to the blank surface until the solder flows. If the flame is directed to the rivet too soon, the solder will flow from the blank surface to the rivet only.

Functional use of rivets
Rivets can be used instead of solder to join blanks together. Take two thin gauge blanks and one flat-headed rivet. Drill a hole in one of the blanks slightly wider in diameter than the shank of the rivet. Now place this blank directly on top of the second blank and, with the drill bit in the hole, drill through the second blank (fig 55a).

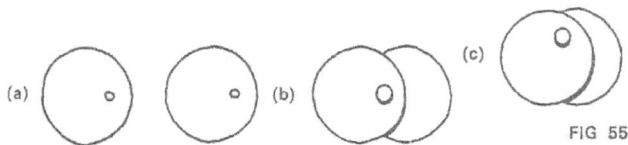

FIG 55

Smooth both surfaces of the blanks and then place the one blank on top of the other with the holes in line with each other. Insert the rivet and twist the blanks to any position, for example, figs 55b,c. When the position is decided, reverse the two blanks and rest the head of the rivet on the steel block with the shank sticking up. Now hold it carefully in position and with the ball end of a chasing hammer, or either end of a ball-pein hammer, begin to hit the end of the shank (fig 56).

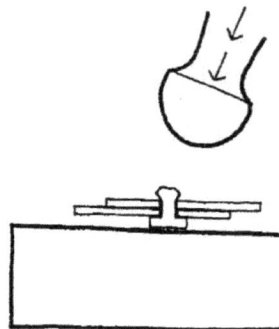

FIG 56

Continue doing this until the shank becomes compressed into a dome-like shape. The shank has now been flattened and has spread out, thus preventing the two blanks from coming apart. If the two blanks can still be *moved,* then the shank has not been sufficiently hammered. They should not move at all.

Great care must be taken to keep the two blanks pressed closely together during the hammering process. If they are allowed to come a little way apart, the bottom part of the shank may begin to spread and it will then be *very* difficult, if not impossible, to get a good join.

When this is complete, smooth the rivet head by turning the compound unit *over* and rubbing the rivet head on emery paper. This compound unit can now be used as a necklace unit or earring. It is also possible to add another blank to it with another rivet. The same advice is offered about trying to determine the joining holes for linking before riveting begins, to enable the smoothing of all surfaces to be done evenly. Quite obviously this is not always possible, for the essence of the constructive process is exploration while the process is continuing. Looking ahead too much can destroy the immediacy of what is being done. It will often be necessary to complete one action before a decision can be taken about the next.

Rivets and perforated metal combination
Take a section of grid no. 1 (see chapter 5) and choose a flat-headed rivet with a shank size which just fits the hole of the grid. Also, the diameter of the head should not be so wide that another rivet cannot be placed in an adjacent hole. You may like to cut out a shape from the grid first and then fill some or all of the holes with the rivets, or shapes can be cut in the grid first and then a few rivets be inserted. For using riveted perforation as units, leave holes open for links (fig 57) and a variation (fig 58).

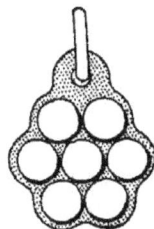
FIG 57

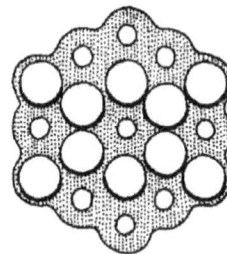
FIG 58

Rivets can of course be used functionally with perforated metal, as pieces can be riveted together in the same way as described for riveting blanks together. With the perforation, the holes are already there and so certain limitations are set. It is a matter of choosing which hole or holes to use. Larger headed rivets can also be used with this size perforation. It means only that they cannot be used adjacent to each other, as the radius of the rivet heads will be greater than half the distance between the centres of any two of the holes. There are many patterns which could be cut from this grid and which could incorporate rivets, and it might help to read the chapter on perforated metals before using the rivets.

Note The stampings, blanks and washers described in this chapter are usually very accurately stamped out, particularly those in pure silver. However, they nearly all need some working, *even* if it is only to smooth the sides of a silver blank. The heavier gauge stampings and blanks show shear marks at the edges. They can easily be removed with a needle file and two or three grades of emery paper.

It should also be noted that the two flat surfaces of all metal stampings - perforated sheets included - are slightly different from each other. The action of the punch downwards on to the metal surface causes a slight rounding of the edges due to compression of the material. The result is shown enlarged in fig 59. This effect increases with the thickness of the metal, and should always be taken into consideration. For example, if two round blanks are to be soldered to each other at their sides, it would be necessary to remove the rounded edges and make the sides vertical from top to bottom. Some burrs from the perforated sheets distort during the punching process (fig 60). This distortion can easily be remedied by placing the burrs individually on the steel block and gently malleting them. Keep reversing until the burr is quite flat.

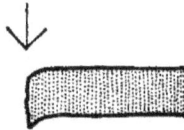

FIG 59

FIG 60

5 · Metal perforation

The process of metal perforation consists of punching out pieces in a sheet of metal to leave a regular grid. This is done by means of a heavy press containing a row of punches which shear out the shapes into dies. The sheet of metal is moved through the press by rollers, and it stops at regular intervals for the row of punches to operate. The punches can be removed and replaced by others, and there is a great variety of different shaped punches. The pieces which fall out of the sheet as a result of the punching are called burrs. These burrs are usually collected and sold as scrap. The industrial uses of perforated metal are numerous and include staircases, floor treads, ventilator and loudspeaker grilles, grading and filtering screens, and office furniture. Many of these grids and burrs can be used creatively, for one may think of a regular, perforated sheet as a collection of units. First let us look at the possibilities of cutting into some of the grids.

Grid no. 1 (fig 61)

FIG 61

The size of the holes in this particular grid can vary considerably, but in the one discussed the diameter of the hole is approximately $1/16$"

Take a saw frame and choose a medium size blade - no. 0. Fix the blade at one end and thread the other through one of the holes in the grid. Fix the blade at the other end in the ordinary way, and proceed to fret out a complete hole with its surrounding metal as in fig 61a. A kind of six-holed star shape will be left (fig 61b). Undo the blade at one end and remove it from the grid. Thread the blade into the next hole along the straight line of holes and proceed to do the same thing. This can be done several times. Now for the moment stop at three star shapes and then proceed to cut them out entirely from the rest of the grid as marked in fig 62.

FIG 62

Great care must be taken not to cut into the fretted pattern, and it is advisable to mark out the shape to be removed by inscribing a line with the end of a needle file or a pointed punch. After the three-star pattern has been completely detached from the rest of the grid, it will be necessary to file along the edges, taking care only to round off the straight edges and to keep the scalloped nature of the pattern. A metal burnisher will give the edges a final polished look.

To smooth both sides of the piece, use a Scotch stone or rub both sides across a fine grade of emery paper which has been placed on the steel block.

You now have a modified grid unit which can be used in many ways.

Thread a link through it (fig 63), and then make a little chain (see chapter 7), fixing it at one end to the link on the unit and at the other end to an ear screw, or use it as a necklace unit (fig 64).

FIG 63

FIG 64

Note: The points which have been cut by the blade will be rather sharp, and it may be necessary to use a triangular or square needle file to smooth the sharp edges. It is also possible to solder this unit on to a flat sheet and then, with a saw, to cut the bottom sheet to the same outside shape (fig 65). This compound unit can now be used as an earring or necklace unit, but a hole or holes will have to be drilled. The holes should be in the same position as the holes in the grid. As there will now be two front surfaces - a top one and a recessed one - it is a nice idea to accentuate them. Do this by dipping the compound unit or units into a solution of potassium sulphide and then highly polishing the top surface. This really throws up the patterned grid in high relief against the recessed blackened surface.

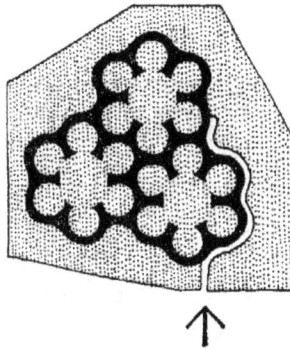

FIG 65

Further patterns

This grid is based on angles of 60° and 120°, and therefore within it can be found equilateral triangles, hexagons, parallelograms and trapezoids. Instead of cutting out the six-point star shape, it is possible to cut at the edge of the star and arrive at a straight edge hexagon. Examination of fig 66 will reveal this and other cutout shapes. Spend some time with a piece of copper grid before attempting to work with silver. There are endless combinations of internal and external shapes you can arrive at in this grid.

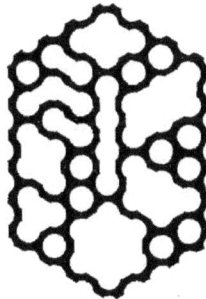

FIG 66

Extended use of grid no. 1

This grid can be used in combination with rivets (see chapter 4).

Grid no. 2 (fig 67)

FIG 67

Most of these grids are stamped out in more than one size, but the width of this particular hole is approximately ¼" Although this grid is more complex than grid no. 1, shapes can be cut from it in the same way.

Thread the saw blade through a hole and cut internal and external shapes as shown in fig 67. Like grid no. 1, this grid can be cut in two directions and the various shapes cut from it can be used in the same way. Depending upon the scale of it, you may have to drill holes into the frames in order to attach links rather than use the existing space through which to thread the links. This particular perforated pattern looks attractive with texturing. It is sometimes worth doing this in order to unify the surface, as the stamping out process is not always quite accurate and sometimes leaves small irregularities which show more in the small scale patterns. Place the cut out unit on the steel block and texture the whole surface with the ball head of a chasing hammer.

Grid no. 3 (fig 68)

FIG 68

The dimensions of the rectangular hole of this grid are 1^1/$_2$" x ¼". Cut out the rectangles with the saw. Smooth the edges and corners with two or three different grades of emery paper and use the burnisher to polish round the edges.
Instead of cutting out the rectangles, the strips can be cut out, as shown in fig 68.

The rectangles
These rectangles make very fine necklace units. Holes should be drilled at the corners and then the units can be joined to each other with links (fig 69).

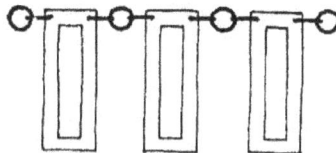

FIG 69

This unit can be slightly modified by curving it. Do this by texturing with the ball head of the chasing hammer, as explained for the previous grid. If one end of the rectangle is held between finger and thumb while hammering, the other end, the rectangle, will gradually curve upwards. This can and should be controlled, and if it curves too much, it can be modified by bending back with the fingers. The material is only textured on one side. If it is attempted on both sides, the action of the hammer on one side negates the previous action on the other side.

The combination of the hammer blows on the top surface and the hard steel block on the underneath surface causes the top surface to become dented or textured and the underneath surface to become hard and flat. If the metal is a fine gauge, signs of the texturing may show on the underneath surface.

The strips
The strips make very good chain units. Depending upon the gauge of the metal, they may need strengthening, as they are very narrow compared with their length. Do this by hammering on the steel block with the flat head of a ball-pein hammer, taking care not to distort the shape of the strip. After smoothing the corners, drill a hole at both ends and join with links. Instead of strengthening the strips in this way, they can be twisted (see page 45) as twisting also hardens the metal. If the gauge is heavy enough, no strengthening is required.

Grid no. 4 (fig 70)

FIG 70

The actual size of the grid is 1$\frac{1}{2}$ times larger than the diagram. This grid pattern was developed by a large firm for use as a radar screen. It is an interesting pattern, and careful examination will show that it is very similar to grid no. 1 and that the propeller-shaped hole can in fact be cut from grid no. 1.
Like the first two grids, many internal and external shapes can be cut from it. Thread a medium saw blade through one of the holes and cut the shapes shown in fig 70 or any others which can be found. These shapes, like those of the previous grids, can be used as necklace units and earrings.

Burrs - grid no. 1 (fig 71)

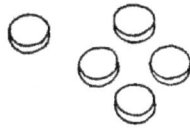

FIG 71

The shapes which drop out from the perforated sheets are just as useful as the frames from which they come. (The word burr should not be confused with the same word used to describe the ridge or ridges which form through compression on the edges of metal.)

These particular burrs, when they are part of a small scale grid, can be soldered on to flat surfaces such as different shaped blanks and stampings. After cleaning the surface of the blank with emery and fluxing it, place the burrs in position. Place small pieces of solder on the flat surface against the burrs and then put the whole piece on the soldering wig. Direct the flame underneath the blank, and only to the top surface at the last moment just as the solder flows. If this is not done correctly, the small burrs will all become soldered to each other, but not at all to the bottom surface.

You can also use these small scale burrs for melting to form equal sized beads or spheres. Take one of them and place it on the charcoal block. Heat it until it turns cherry red, and then continue heating a little more until it begins to draw into itself. As it reaches melting point, it will form into a sphere. If the burr is placed on a flat part of the charcoal block, there is a danger that as it forms into a sphere it will begin to roll off the block; or, if it remains in position, it will not form a perfect sphere but will have a flat bottom. One way of avoiding both these things is to make a small hemispherical depression in the charcoal block. Do this by twisting a doming punch into the surface of the block. Take a size slightly larger than the diameter of the burr, or whichever size helps form the sphere. Experiment may be necessary. Do not twist the punch into the charcoal block too vigorously or the block will crack in half.

Constructing with round blanks – burrs

FIG 72

With this burr and a larger round blank, you can make a construction as shown in fig 72. This may look like a difficult operation, but if tackled step by step it can be achieved. Start by preparing the surfaces of four burrs and three larger round blanks by using emery paper in the usual way.

Place the small burr on the first blank as shown in fig 73a and solder it in position. Then turn the piece upside down, place the next burr in position (fig 73b) and solder that by directing the flame on to the top surface only. Now keeping the same position, place the next blank underneath (fig 73c). Direct the flame carefully and the piece will not fall apart.

The next stage will mean balancing the piece on the small burr (fig 73d). Do this by placing the piece on a charcoal block with a small piece of charcoal at either side as supports, or place the whole piece on the soldering wig.

The next step is to place the whole piece on the third blank, supporting it with charcoal each side, and solder that in position. The final soldering operation will mean turning the piece upside down again and soldering the fourth burr in position. If this construction is small enough, use it as an earring. Attach a link to it by soldering a small, round, hollow section to one end (fig 73e). If this construction is larger, it can hang as a pendant.

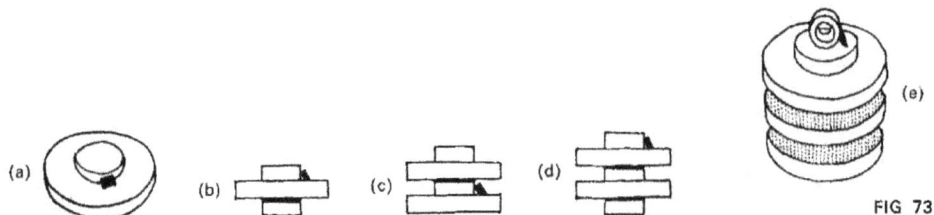

FIG 73

Burrs - grid no. 2 (fig 74)

FIG 74

These units on a small scale can also be used to solder on to flat surfaces such as different shaped blanks. For finishing, blacken in potassium sulphide and highly polish top surfaces.

Burrs - grid no. 3 (fig 75a)

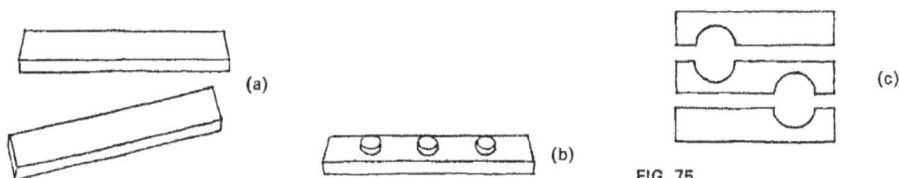

FIG 75

Heavy chain units can be made with these burrs. Drill a hole at both ends and then link them together or make a small chain to go between them (see chapter 7). They can also be used as the flat surfaces on which to solder burrs from grid nos 1 and 2 (fig 75b). This unit is also large enough to modify in various ways. Take a saw and fret out semicircular shapes as shown in fig 75c. These pieces can be related to each other vertically as a pendant, or they can still be used as chain units. The shape of this burr can also be extended. Cut into the ends with the fret-saw as shown in fig 76a and then bend the legs in any direction (fig 76b).

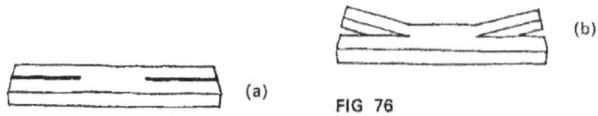

(a)

(b)

FIG 76

Burrs - grid no. 4
These burrs can be used for earrings or necklace units and can be soldered on to flat surfaces. They can also be riveted together to form interesting structures (fig 77).

FIG 77

Note The uses of these burrs will vary depending on the scale of the grid. For example, the burr from grid no. 2 can be used as a chain unit or a necklace unit if it is large enough (fig 78). Grid no. 1 on a larger scale would provide a larger round blank as its burr, but might render the frame too large for use in jewelry making. Burrs from grid no. 3 can be considered as rectangular blanks.

Finally, these burrs come into the category of stampings and blanks, and should be handled in the same way, particularly when they are on a large scale (see chapter 4).

6 · Some handmade units

Even with so many ready-made units available, it is often necessary and desirable to make units by hand. The most often used handmade unit is the link. Even so, these links can be bought in certain sizes and are then called jump rings. They are available in brass, copper, silver and gold.

Link making
Take a hand drill and fix it horizontally in a bench vice in such a way that the drill may be freely rotated. Take a steel rod $1/8$" diameter and place it into the three-jaw chuck of the drill (fig 79).

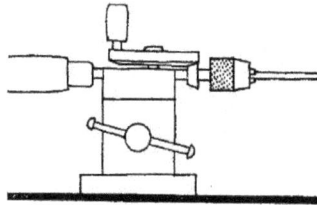

FIG 79

Now take a length of wire and make a right-angled bend at one end. Hook this short end into any one of the spaces between the three jaws of the chuck (fig 80).

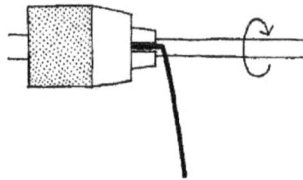

FIG 80

The length of wire should pass over the front of the steel rod. Now grip the steel rod with the right hand as if it were a pencil, placing the thumb on the section of wire which passes over the rod. With the left hand, slowly turn the handle of the drill so that the rod revolves in the direction indicated in the figure. The wire will begin to wind up on the rod to make a coil. Guide the wire with the thumb so that the coil is as tight as it can be. When the length of wire is used up, the coil can be pulled off the right end of the rod. If the short wire piece seems stuck in the chuck jaw, release the whole rod and the coil will then easily slip off the left side. The coil or spring should look like fig 81.

FIG 81

Cutting off the links from a coil

Take the coil in the left hand and hold it vertically between the thumb and first finger, on the inside of the hand, with the coil nearest the body. Press the thumb and first finger with the coil against the bench pin on the workbench. Take the saw and, with the blade in vertical line with the coil, begin to saw at the top of the coil (fig 82).

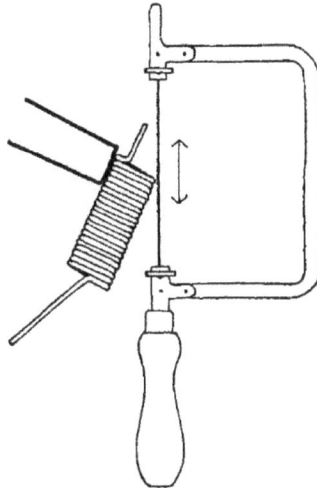

FIG 82

As the blade cuts through the top of the coil, the first link will come away. Always keep that part of the coil which is being cut tightly held between the thumb and first finger. Any movement might cause the blade to bend in the wrong direction and thus to break.

Continue to saw until the coil has been completely cut away into links. The finer the blade used to cut the links, the more easily the links will close. The links cut with a fine blade will look as in fig 83, and if the links are cut with a thicker blade, they will look as in fig 84a. This link, when closed, will look as in fig 84b, and it can be seen that this is not the best kind of join for soldering. The blade size can vary according to the gauge of the wire, but it must never cut away more than a minute segment of the circle. The links are now ready to use.

FIG 83

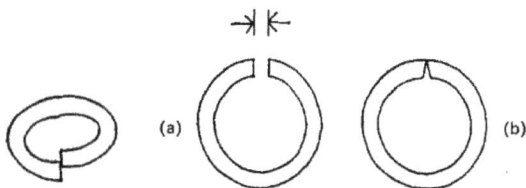

(a)   (b)

FIG 84

Determining sizes

The inside diameter of the link should correspond to the diameter of the steel rod used for winding up the coil. However, this will only be true if the wire used is soft. If the wire is semi-hard or hard, a certain amount of spring will occur, so that when the thumb is removed after winding on the coil, the tension will be released and the coil will expand.

The amount of expansion depends on the hardness of the wire. This means that if an exact link size is required, an allowance will have to be made for the spring. Practice will show how much this is.

It is very useful to keep a set of steel rods of varying sizes for link making and experience will show which sizes are most used.

A note on standardizing

In theory there is an infinite number of link sizes in relation to wire gauges, and there seems to be no good reason for using arbitrary and varying sizes each time one needs links. After some experience, it is a good idea to fix on three or four different wire gauges. They should be standard sizes - that is to say, sizes which can be bought. Generally it is a waste of time making wire when it can be so readily bought. The same is true of hollow sections and many of the units described in this book, all of which can be made by hand. But we must remember that our work only begins at the point where the machine stops.

Practice and experience will show a preference for three or four different gauges and a limited number of link sizes. Keep unused links sorted in sizes and gauges. They will always be needed, particularly when standard sizes are in use.

Re-shaping soldered links

Once links have been soldered, they can be reshaped in many different ways. The shaping is mostly done with pliers. Here are a few examples.

Take a round soldered link, inside diameter ¼" - that is, made on rod no. 7 - and gauge ·036". Take a pair of round-nosed pliers and insert the points into the link. Now pull the pliers apart slowly with both hands and the link will gradually stretch to an oblong shape (fig 85).

FIG 85

The link joint can either be in the middle or at the end, although the end is preferable, as the two sides will then show no unevenness. The joining link will *cover* the joint at the end, which, in any case, should be as neat and unobtrusive as possible. This is achieved by using the correct amount of solder. A thin oblong is made by stretching the link at the narrow end of the nose and a fatter oblong farther along the nose. To make an oblong link when the original round link is too small for the pliers to be inserted, use a pair of parallel pliers and squeeze the link together. This action may also be necessary in conjunction with the other process just described: using the parallel pliers after the first stretching process has begun often helps to give the oblong unit a better and more *even* shape.

Note: It is absolutely essential that the links are properly soldered, otherwise they will surely come apart during the stretching process.

Extensions of the oblong modification
With the round nosed pliers still inserted after the stretching process, take a flat-nosed pair of pliers and press the two sides of the oblong together so that the link looks as in fig 86a.
Or, with the round-nosed pliers inserted, take another pair of round-nosed pliers and just squeeze the sides of the oblong together at one point only. This works well with a smaller link. For a larger link, push the link farther up the pliers before nipping in the middle (fig 86b).

(a)   (b)

FIG 86

Flattening soldered links
The round or modified link shapes can be flattened for extended uses. This is done by placing them on the steel block and using a ball-pein hammer. Or if a little irregularity is preferred, use the ball head of the chasing hammer which will cause texturing. The oblong link may need a little reshaping afterwards. This can be done with the parallel pliers as previously described.

Further uses of flattened links
Apart from chain units, these flattened links can be used in bas-relief in the same way as hollow sections (see page 28). In this case it will be necessary to have the bottom surface of the link flat and smooth. Do this in the usual way by rubbing it across emery paper on a steel block. After this preparation, flux the surface where the link will be soldered and place the link unit or units in position. Place small pieces of solder on the inside surface, close against the sides of the link. Place on the soldering wig and heat very gently from underneath until the flux has bubbled. Then, with the probe, make sure the link units are in position and are quite flat on the surface. Intensify the heat until the solder flows, at which point concentrate the flame on the top surface. It should be possible to see the solder flowing all along the inside and outside edges. When this happens, it means that the link units are properly soldered on.
If the solder does not flow easily round all the edges, use the probe to draw it. Drop in acid and rinse in water. It sometimes happens that a small residue of solder is left where the pieces of solder were originally placed, or that although the solder has run, it has also 'eaten' into the surface where it was placed. The result of either of these things is a kind of 'pock marked' surface. This surface cannot be smoothed down successfully with emery paper, and the best way of achieving a clean surface is to use a Scotch stone. Take the smallest stone and after dipping into water, place it vertically on the surface inside the link where the marks are located. Rub backwards and forwards, or in a circular motion, using more water when it begins to dry. This will gradually grind down the surface until it is even and smooth.
If the Scotch stone is too large to fit into the space, shape it as much as necessary by placing a piece of medium grade emery paper on the flat surface of the bench and rubbing the stone backwards and forwards across it. The end of the stone can thus be sharpened to any required shape.
These flat link units can be soldered on to any flat surface.

Other useful units to make
If you use a very fine gauge metal, it is quite simple to cut out some regular or irregular shapes with the hand shears. Take a very thin sheet of silver or copper, say a sheet 6" x 1". Cut it into regular strips ¼" wide, which makes twenty-four one-inch strips. Drill a hole at either end and this unit now becomes a very useful chain unit (fig 87). If the metal is soft, it will need to be hardened by hammering. Use the flat head of the ball-pein hammer, or its ball-head if texturing is preferred. Use emery paper for smoothing off sharp corners.

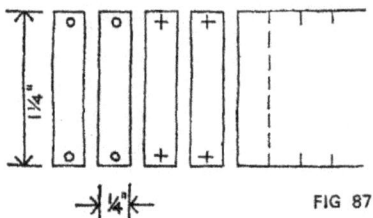

FIG 87

Many shapes can be cut from a flat sheet, but we have already seen what is available in stampings and blanks and there is no point in making by hand what can more accurately be stamped. The reason for choosing a very fine gauge for the occasional handmade unit is that they can easily be cut and one can then experience the difference of using units which do not have machine accuracy.
Finally, any amount of handmade units can be cut out or moulded, but it is not the intention here to explore this matter. This book is mainly concerned with using and modifying ready-made units. What units you may come to make yourself will probably depend on what discoveries you make while using the ready-made units.

7 · Units and chains

A chain is a collection of units strung together in a line. Both its length and content are infinitely variable. A chain hanging round the neck and a unit necklace are interchangeable, the one can easily become the other. Where the unit is itself compounded of many parts, you may prefer to let the 'chain' rest round the neck, as a longer one may become too heavy. Otherwise, there is no particular reason why one should stop the chain at 15" rather than 28", 30" or 32" - all possible chain lengths. The point is, when the 'chain' is 15"-16" long and fits round the neck, it is called a necklace. When it is longer and hangs down, it is usually called a chain. Several small links joining larger units together are also known as chain lengths. However, our concern is with content and structure not with form. First, a study of the parts and how they can be put together, and only then what is to be done with the structure. There are times when you should keep the final purpose in mind, and with certain necklaces this is admittedly necessary.

This chapter will show how many of the units which have been described can be considered as chain units. The chains can also become necklaces.

The round blank
Take sixteen round blanks 1" in diameter and drill two holes at either end (fig 88).

FIG 88

Prepare the surfaces to the finish required. Take some links not larger than $1/4$" diameter, thread them through the holes and close them. To join these sixteen units together, make a short length of link chain to go between them. Make this length the same as the diameter of the blank. If the link diameter is $1/4$", this means you will need four links. However, the number of links in a chain determines the direction in which the unit will hang in relation to the next unit. That is to say, an odd number of links - one, three, five, seven and so on - will mean that the round blanks will lie in the same direction (fig 89). But an even number of links, two, four, six, eight, means that the units will hang at right-angles to each other. Sometimes you may want the main units of a chain to hang in opposition to each other, but in this case, the main units - the round blanks - will lie in the same direction and so there will be five links in the joining chain and not four.

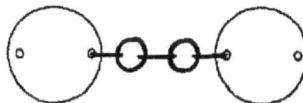

FIG 89

The simplest way of making the joining chain is to take a link for the centre position and close it so that you now have the blanks with their side links and one for the middle (fig 90).

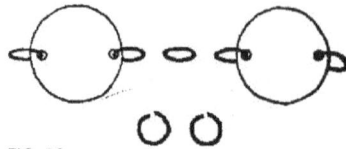

FIG 90

Now take two more links and with them join the centre link to the links attached to the two blanks. Do this with the remaining seven pairs of blanks. Then, join up the pairs to make fours and so on until all the blanks are joined to each other and there are just two ends to the chain.

To join the two ends, hold the top link, which should be open, in a pair of flat nosed pliers and let the chain hang down. Follow the chain down with the other hand, making sure the blanks are hanging correctly in the same direction and that the joining chain is not twisted. Now hold the bottom link in another pair of pliers and, without twisting the chain, bring it up to meet the open link at the top of the chain; slip it on and close the link. You now have a complete chain which can hang round the neck.

Note: If precious metal is used, soldering the links is advised.

Same chain with machine-made joining chain

It is possible to buy link chain which is made by machine. This is available in brass, copper, copper-plated brass, silver and gold. The links are soldered and the chain can be cut off at any length. These link chains are available in various sizes and patterns, and some firms supply illustrated catalogues.

The chain just described can be made with lengths of machine-made chain as the joining link chain. Choose a pattern and size and cut off an inch length. Be sure to count the links before cutting so that there is an odd number, although this may mean that the chain will be a little longer or shorter than an inch. As the links of the machine-made chain are soldered, this link chain will now be joined to the blank with a handmade link (fig 91). The addition of two handmade links will increase the overall length of the joining chain, and therefore you may like to cut off a shorter length of machine-made chain to allow for it.

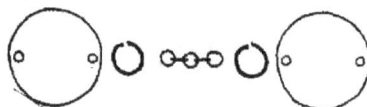

FIG 91

Note: It is also possible to buy ready-made open links in copper, brass, silver and gold. They are called 'jump' rings. They are available in various gauges and sizes, and it is often worth buying and keeping a selection of them when working in copper or brass. In precious metals, however, it is better to make them by hand, as they are relatively more expensive to buy.

Other blank shapes as chain units

The rectangular blank or burr from grid no. 2 (see chapter 5) is an obvious chain unit.

Deal with it in the same way as the round blank (fig 92). If the rectangle is narrow and a fine gauge, it can be modified by twisting (fig 93). Drill holes at either end for joining, and prepare all the surfaces. Then hold each end of the strip with flat-nosed pliers and twist once or twice, or more times, depending on the softness of the metal. It will begin to crack if it is twisted too much.

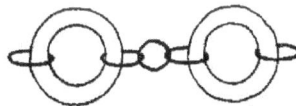

FIG 92

FIG 93

Note: The end surfaces can lie in the same direction or at right-angles to each other, the principle being the same as described for link directions.

Washers as chain units (fig 94)

The existing hole in a washer can be used for linking one to the other. Or, if the diameter of the washer is large in proportion to the hole, it may be necessary to drill two further holes, otherwise the joining link would need to be too large (fig 94).

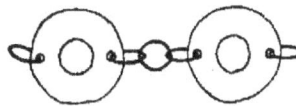

FIG 94

Hollow sections as chain units

Most hollow sections can be used very successfully for chain units, the most obvious ones being cut round hollow sections (fig 95). They should be smoothed, polished and deburred before joining. Rectangular hollow sections also make very good chain units (fig 96), as well as oval and fluted sections.

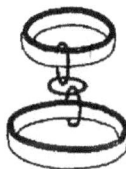

FIG 95

FIG 96

Flattening hollow sections

If the hollow sections are cut thin enough, it is possible to flatten them by hammering on the steel block.

This may be considered unnecessary for round hollow sections, as the same effect can be achieved by flattening round soldered links as described in chapter 6. However, there is a difference in the detail of these two flattened units which is noticeable on a large scale. The flattened hollow section will not have such a rounded side as the flattened link.

Experiment will show this. The flattened rectangular, oval and fluted hollow sections will provide fairly regular 'closed' links of these shapes, which would otherwise be difficult to make.

Links as primary chain units
We have already seen that links are an essential part of a chain. They can also be used as the visually dominant units.

Make links ¾" in diameter and $^1/_{16}$" gauge. Close them and they can now be used, like the thin hollow sections, as the primary chain units, joined to each other with smaller links (fig 97).

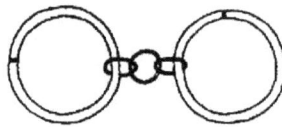

FIG 97

If they are to be flattened by hammering, they must be soldered, otherwise the hammering will distort the shape, causing the ends to separate. When soldering copper links, use 18 carat yellow gold solder. The colour combination is pretty, and it gives an added warmth and a more precious quality to the copper. This is approaching decoration through function.

Unit combinations in chains
The variety of unit combinations in chains is infinite. However, the most successful and simple chains are those which do not have more than two different primary units. This is because it is difficult to relate too many different shapes to each other. The one detracts from the other so that the visual clarity of the parts is destroyed by too much variation. After all, even a chain composed of two primary units still has small link units which could compete with them.

Some clear combinations are the rectangle and circle together (fig 98). The rectangle could be twisted, which gives it a three-dimensional quality; to match this depth, use a similar width hollow section as the circular unit.

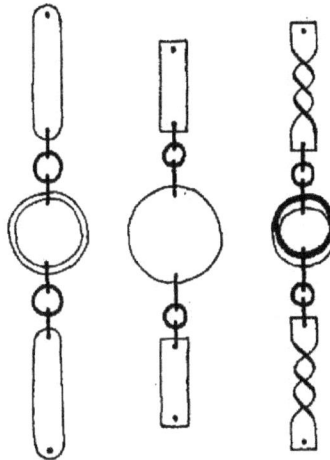

FIG 98

Links as chain units

You may like to make a single unit chain composed only of links. Make a series of links from ·036" silver or copper wire on rod no. 7 (see chapter 6). Cut them through with a fine saw blade and solder the first ten. Use 18 carat yellow gold solder for copper. Now, with the round-nosed pliers, stretch them as shown on page 66. There will now be ten oblong links.

Take a round unsoldered link and thread it through two of the oblong links. Solder it and then stretch it in the same way as before. Take care not to damage the other two, already stretched, links. Use as many links as necessary to make up the desired length of chain, which will then be a repeated unit chain (fig 99).

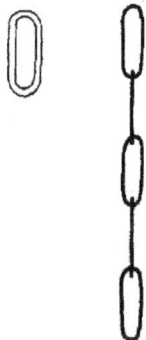

FIG 99

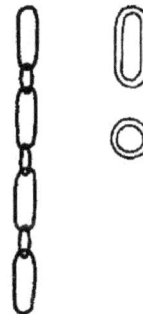

FIG 100

For a slight variation, make two sizes of links, say rod no. 3 with rod no. 7. Solder the smaller links first in this case, and with the parallel pliers squeeze them to an oblong shape as described on page 42. Now thread the large link between two smaller ones and, after soldering, stretch it as before. Continue making a length with alternate sized links. The chain will be similar to the preceding one, with a smaller second unit. The smaller link could be left circular, which is another variation (fig 100).

Grid no. 1 as chain units

Sections of this grid can make excellent chain units, for example, a one line strip of holes of any length. These lengths can be modified by cutting through some of the holes but leaving two holes at either end for joining. Or the six-hole star shape can be cut out, plus two extra holes for joining the unit. Any shape which can be cut from this grid is a potential chain unit.

Matching chains with pendants

Having finished making a pendant, and after deciding how and from which point or points it should hang, you are then faced with choosing a chain for it.

The best way to approach this is first to decide whether or not to use one or more of the units in the pendant. Remember that the pendant is the main object and that the chain is only a form of mounting - like the frame of a painting. This analogy is instructive, for a good framer will always take care never to make the frame detract from the painting. He may elaborate and even paint the frame, perhaps using a small amount of a colour used in the painting. Nevertheless, if the frame, by its colour, embellishments or scale, overpowers the painting, it has failed as a frame. So in 'mounting' pendants, you must keep the same questions in mind.

If you decide against using any of the units in the pendant because they perhaps compete too much with it, you can relate the chain in some other way. For example, if the overall structure of the pendant is dense, you may prefer to have an openwork chain. Or the reverse may be the case. There are no rules except those which you invent for yourself. The point to remember is that the final choice must show off the pendant to its best advantage.

Length of chain for pendants

The length of chain for a pendant is a personal choice which can be related to the wearer. However, a pendant which is flat one side – bas-relief or both sides – cut-out can hang higher up the body, resting on it. A more sculptural or three-dimensional pendant should hang more freely, that is, lower down the body.

As stated, the possible variations in chain making are quite enormous, and when using a new unit one should always think of its possible use as a chain unit.

Polishing Chains

The polishing of chains can most easily be done in the following way: take a round wooden rod, say 4" in length and approximately ¼" in diameter. Fix it vertically into the bench vice with about 2" submerged. Loop the chain over the rod and stretch it out towards you with one hand, and with the other take a piece of soft leather. After applying some Tripoli to it, proceed to wrap it around one length of the chain and rub it backwards and forwards along the length. Alter the position of the chain around the wooden rod until all the surfaces of the chain have been polished. Take another piece of soft leather and do the same thing with the polishing rouge. After both these actions, immerse the chain in a little paraffin and brush it with a bristle brush to remove excess rouge or Tripoli. Then wash well with a soft brush in warm soapy water.

Note: Do not pull the chain too tightly towards you or the units around the wooden rod may distort. If any of the units in the chain are links with a diameter greater than ¼", it will be possible to hook one of them over the rod. All chains can be polished in this way, and the rubbing action will naturally vary according to the type of units in the chain. A chain of small, oblong links will be polished much more easily and quickly than a chain compounded of rectangular blanks and round hollow sections.

"It is not easy to arrive at a conception of a whole which is constructed from parts belonging to different dimensions. And not only nature, but also Art, her transformed image, is such a whole."

Paul Klee
In
Paul Klee on Modern Art
Faber & Faber

Plate 1: Adenovirus

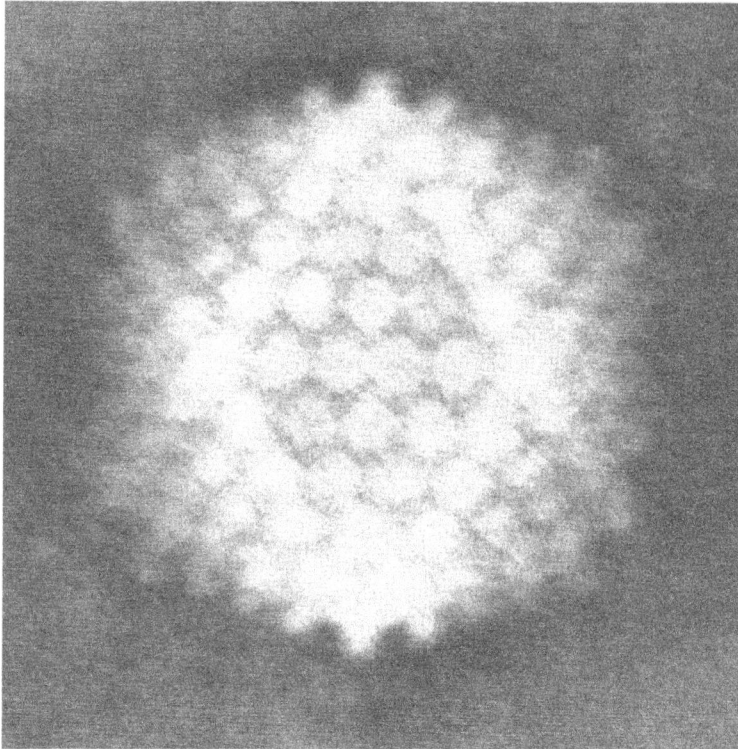

Size / diameter, 0·080 micron (1 micron equals 0.001 millimeter)

This virus is known to cause conjunctivitis, sore throats and feverish colds. The photograph shows its overall shape to be an icosahedron (20 triangular faces) and that the surface is composed of 252 molecules, the small white circles. Note how each molecule is surrounded by six others, like the pattern of grid no. 1, except at the apices of each triangle where the common molecule is surrounded by only five others. Neither the internal structure nor the structure of the individual molecules is yet known.

The photograph was taken through an electron microscope, and as reproduced is magnified 1,000,000 times.

Plate 2:
Pendant and Chain
Photo: Tony Stone

Size: 4³/₄" x 1¹/₂"
Material: standard silver
Main units: hollow sections and rectangular blanks

This pendant is one in a series. It is an invented form whose content can vary considerably.

The hollow sections which are cut to similar lengths have been soldered to the burrs from grid no. 3 in a repeated order - that is, three on the top line and two at the bottom. Naturally the differences in dimensions of the units alter the exactness of their positions, but the system remains fairly clear nevertheless.

There are six different shaped sections, and each group of five is repeated three times in the same order, thus giving a total of eighteen compound units. The chain units are round links and modified oblong links. The round links are of a heavier gauge, to give the chain more strength as the pendant is heavy. The pendant and chain have been blackened and the top surfaces highly polished.

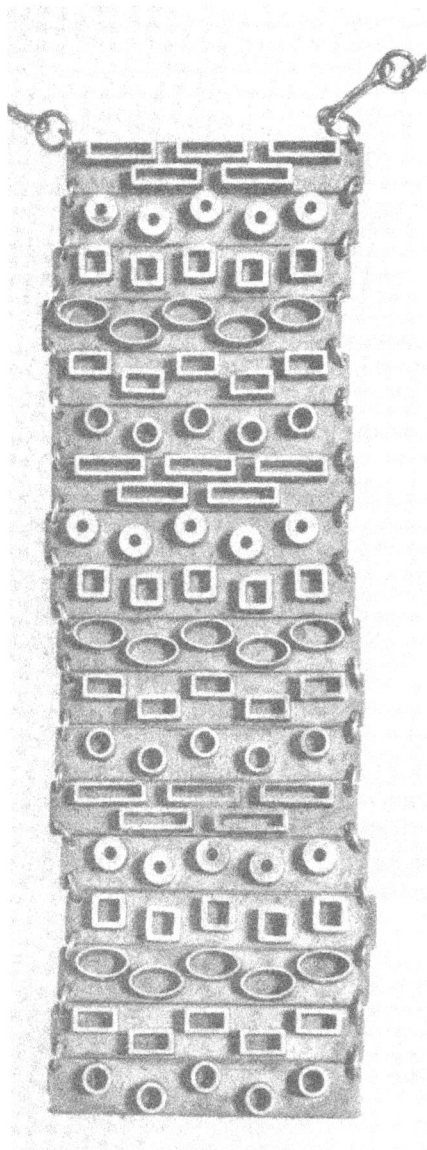

Plate 3:
Pendant and Chain
Photo: Photo Studios Ltd

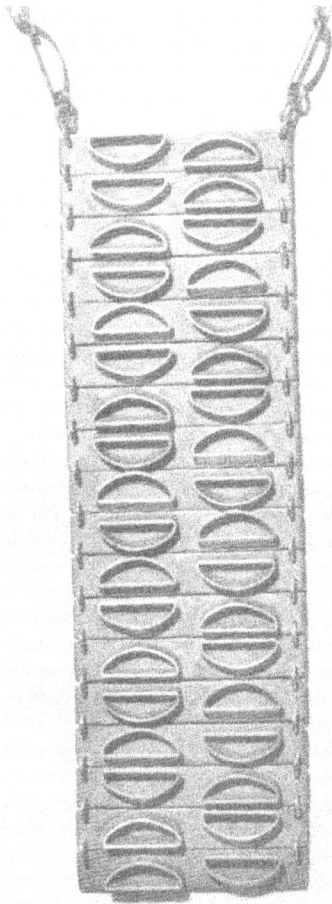

FIG 101

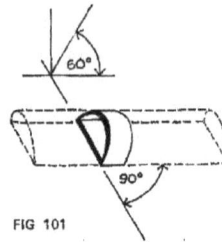

Size: 4³/₄" x 1¹/₂"
Material: standard silver
Main units: semicircular hollow sections and rectangular blanks
The rectangular blanks in this pendant, like the other related pendants, are burrs from grid no. 3. The units placed on them are curved hollow sections, which are not quite halfround, and they have been cut off at an angle of approximately 60° in the plane shown in fig 101.

They have been arranged in the following way: assuming a fixed viewing position and that the unit is placed face down with its straight edge parallel to the length of the rectangle, it will be found that there are four different aspects. They have been repeatedly used throughout the work, and the units have also been placed in varying vertical relationships to each other. The second half of the pendant, from row ten onwards, is the same as the first half, but the repetition begins from the middle point and works downwards in a diagonal way. That is to say, the right-hand unit in row nine is similarly placed to the left-hand unit in row ten; the left-hand unit in row nine is similarly placed to the right-hand unit in row ten. The same is true for rows eight and eleven, seven and twelve, and so on. Also, the first two rows in the pendant are similar, as are the last two rows. These repeated lines top and bottom produce a 'stop' at both ends; they contain the system within them. The chain consists of right-angled cuts of the same hollow section. Note that they can hang in either direction (fig 102).

FIG 102

Plate 4:
Pendant and chain
Photo: Tony Stone

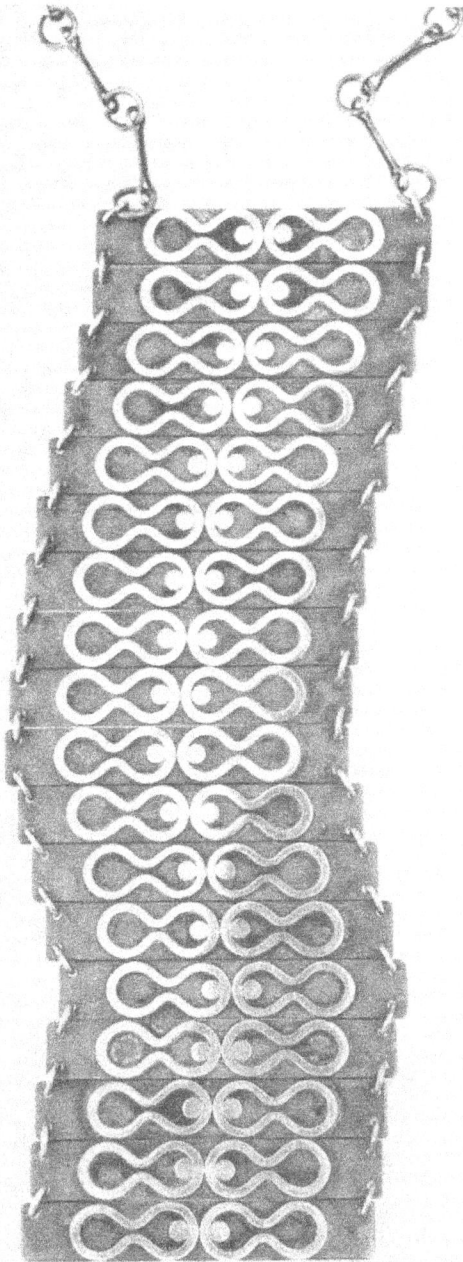

Size: $4^3/_4$" x $1^1/_2$"
Material: standard silver
Main units:

- rectangular burrs from grid no. 3
- small round burrs from grid no. 1
- modified link units

Modified link units were flattened and smoothed on both sides, and the small round burrs on one side. All four units on each rectangular blank were soldered in position at the same time, after the four holes had been drilled. The rectangular blanks were then placed with the units down on to emery paper, and abraded until all the applied units were the same level. {The gauge of the grid from which the small burrs came was heavier than the gauge of the flattened link unit.) The compound units were finished by using scotch stone, fine emery paper and then the hand-polishing stick. The chain is open in design to counteract the density of the pendant.

The whole pendant and chain was subsequently dipped in a solution of potassium sulphide for blackening and then the top surfaces were highly polished.

Plate 5:
Pendant and chain
Photo: Tony Stone

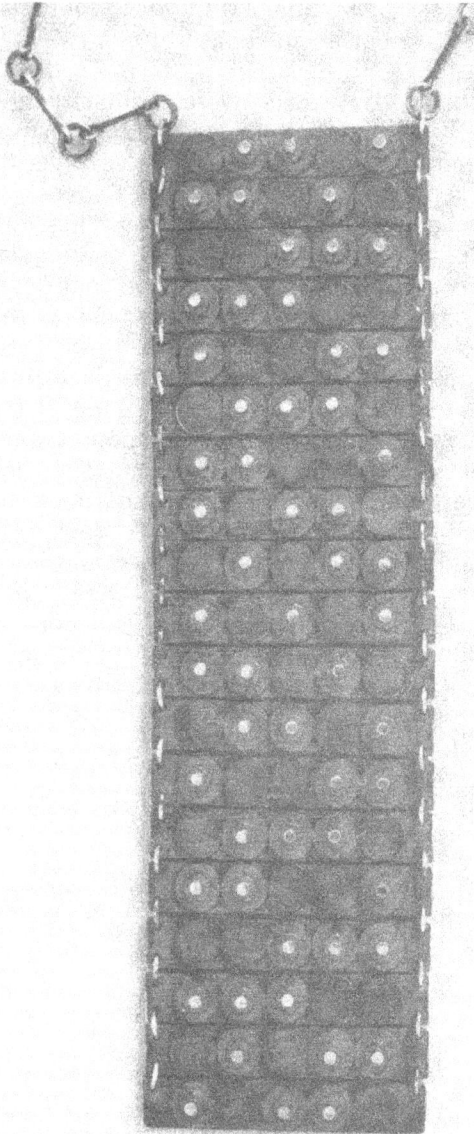

Size: 5" x 1$^{1}/_{2}$"
Material: Fine and standard silver
Main units: rectangles, round blanks, flat-headed rivets

The rectangles are burrs from grid no. 3. The compound units were made by soldering five round blanks on to each rectangle, and. three flat-headed rivets heads down on to the centres of three selected round blanks, leaving two blanks without rivets.

If one makes such a decision - that is to say, a decision to fix a lesser number of units on to a larger number of other units - one can examine all the possible variations. The quantities of these variations are listed in Pascal's Pyramid. This is a series of numbers arranged in a triangular grid (fig 103).

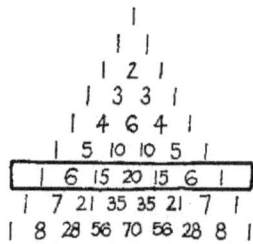

```
          |
         |  |
        |  2  |
       |  3  3  |
      |  4  6  4  |
     |  5  10  10  5  |
   | 6  15  20  15  6  |
  | 7  21  35  35  21  7  |
 | 8  28  56  70  56  28  8 |
| 9  36  84  126  126  84  36  9 |
```

FIG 103

The arrangement of the number allows one to read off all possible variations, for example, of a given number of units in a given number of boxes. Say you have six boxes with two units to place in them. Look for the sixth horizontal row of numbers -the framed row in the diagram - as this is the relevant line. To the left of six is a number one, and this number indicates the situation when there are no units at all to place in the six boxes. The answer is only one variation. The second number in the line - number six - indicates that when there is one unit to place in the six boxes, the answer is six variations. The third number along indicates what the variation is when there are two units to place in six boxes - fifteen variations. The fourth number along indicates the variation when there are three units to place in six boxes - twenty variations. Note that the triangle is symmetrical. This is because, taking the same example, two units placed in six boxes have the same number of combinations as four units placed in six boxes (fig 104).

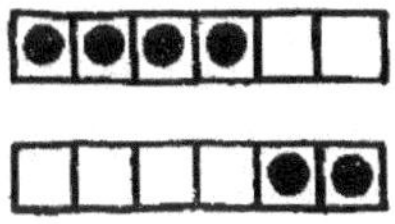

FIG 104

In the case of the illustrated pendant, if you look along row five of the triangle, you will see that when there are three units to place in five boxes, the variation is ten possibilities. The ten rectangles of the pendant show these ten variations. The eleventh row is the reverse of row nine; the twelfth row is the reverse of row eight and so on. The tenth row is common to both parts of the pendant. This means that there are nineteen rectangular compound units, also that nine variations only are repeated.

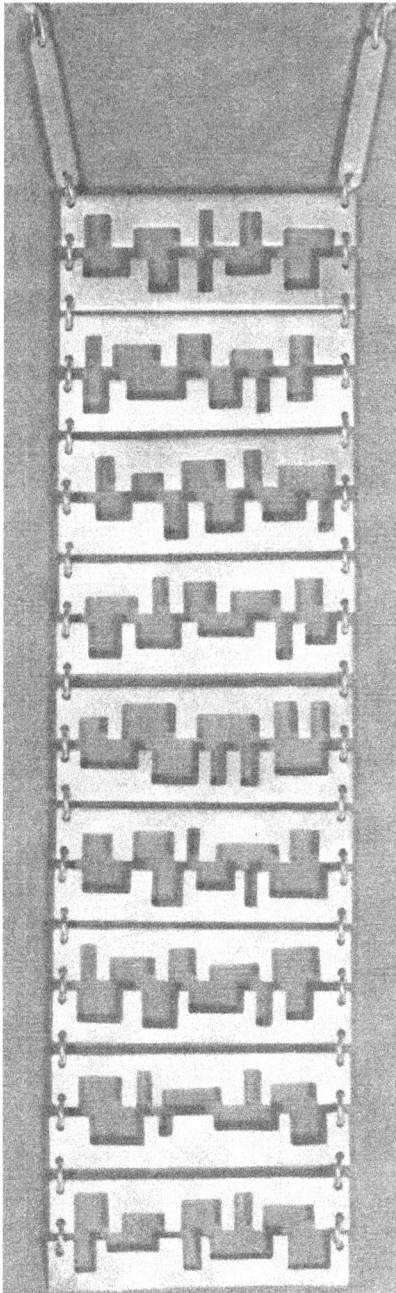

Size: $4^3/_4$" x $1^1/_2$"
Material: Standard silver
Main units: burrs from grid no. 3

These burrs have been modified by cutting into them along one of their lengths. There are five cutouts in each one, and the cutouts of the pairs are related to each other as shown in the six pairs of open rectangles in fig 105. There are many more variations than are explored in this pendant.

FIG 105

The chain is composed of sections of the frame of the same grid. The long strips have been cut into halves and the corners have been slightly rounded. The whole piece has been brightened with a fine brass wire brush.

Plate 7:
Pendant and chain
Photo: Photo Studios Ltd

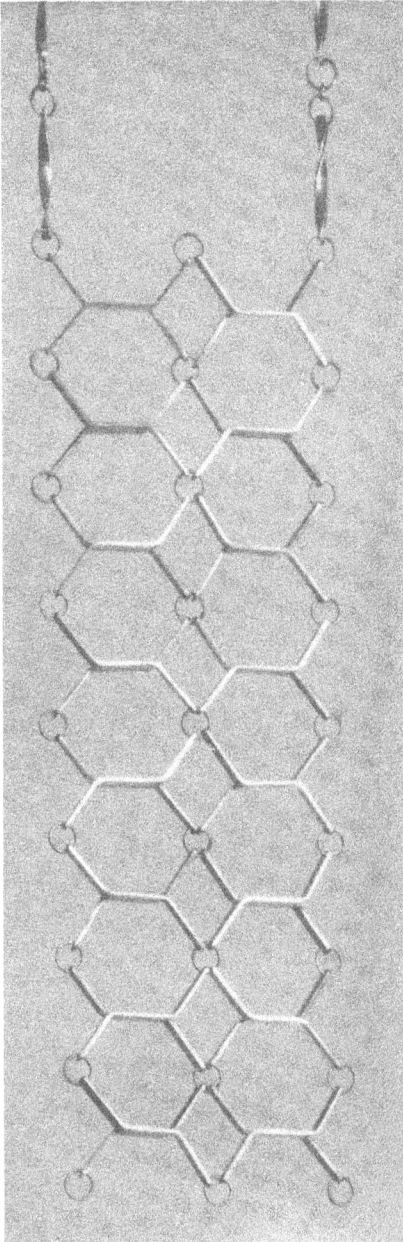

Size: 7$\frac{1}{4}$" x 2$\frac{1}{2}$"
Material: standard silver; chain units of fine silver
Main units: burrs from grid no. 3, rectangular stampings

As described in chapter 5, the shape of these burrs or rectangular blanks can be extended by cutting into each end and bending the 'legs'. Many flat shapes can be treated in a similar way, and this particular kind of unit modification is a whole study in itself.

Note that by cutting one third of the way into each end, the 'legs' can be bent at 120 ° and so form a hexagon when placed together with another similarly modified unit. Each unit in the horizontal pair is in mirror opposition to the other. This gives an added complexity to the top linear surfaces by delineating a larger scale figure and pattern.

The long units in the chain are made of two twisted rectangles. These units are in fine silver and in a fine gauge. To give them greater strength, it was decided to twist them and to use two. The pendant and chain were subsequently blackened and the top surfaces highly polished, which accentuates the larger pattern.

Plate 8:
Pendant and chain
Photo: Tony Stone

Size: 5$\frac{1}{2}$" x 1"
Material: fine silver and standard silver
Main units: electrical contacts (fig 106)

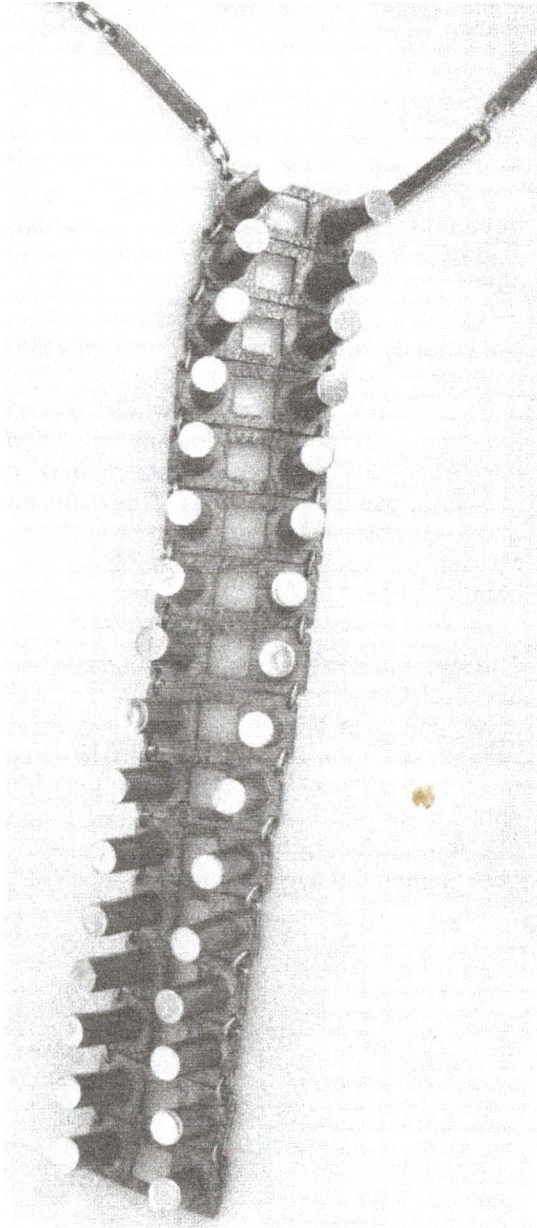

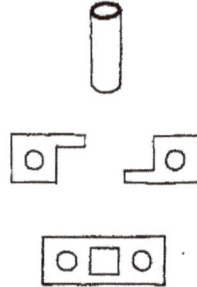

FIG 106

The hollow cups were placed with their openings over the holes in the flat compound units. After this, each unit, now compounded of two L-shapes and two hollow cups, was placed on the steel block, and the flat surfaces were textured with a small size doming punch. This was necessary as a hardening process, the flat units being in fine silver which was annealed by the soldering process. The chain units were taken from the strips of grid no. 3, and were cut in half to provide an appropriate length to scale with the pendant units.

Finally, the piece was blackened and the top flat surfaces of the hollow cups highly polished.

Plate 9:
Pendant and chain
Photo: Photo Studios Ltd

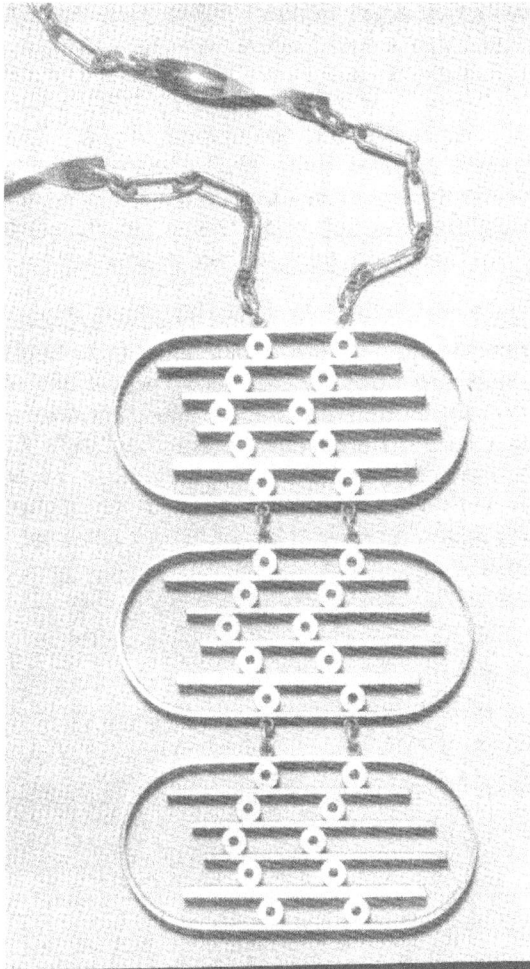

Size: 3¹/₂" x 2¹/₄"
Material: standard silver
Main units: large oval hollow sections, round hollow sections, rectangular blanks

If you begin with a large enough hollow section, all kinds of complex constructions can be made within it. In this case, the whole compound unit is repeated three times, and although each one is complete and self-contained, they have been placed together in a way which unifies the separate compound units. This is achieved by letting the lines, which are formed by the arrangement of the round hollow sections, run into each other. This vertical arrangement counteracts the otherwise powerful horizontal effect of the compound units. The horizontal rectangular blanks are burrs from grid no. 3, and the thicker horizontal at the bottom of each oblong section is two burrs soldered together. The chain also has rectangular pieces in it, and they are twisted once, giving them a depth which approximately matches that of the compound units.

Note the positions of the small round hollow sections to which the chain ends are attached. These positions seem to be the only possible ones along the top horizontal, as anywhere else would introduce two new vertical lines into the pendant when attaching the chain ends.

Note: The period between finishing the three separate compound units and joining them together was approximately eighteen months. It sometimes happens that when compound units are finished, the way to put them together is not immediately clear. One should lay them aside and look at them regularly. At some point, the current work will indicate, by its similar nature or in some other way, a method of dealing with them, even though it may take eighteen months to happen.

Plate 10:
Necklace
Photo: Photo Studios Ltd

Size: outside diameter of large, round hollow section – $^7/_8$"
Material: standard silver
Main units: round hollow sections

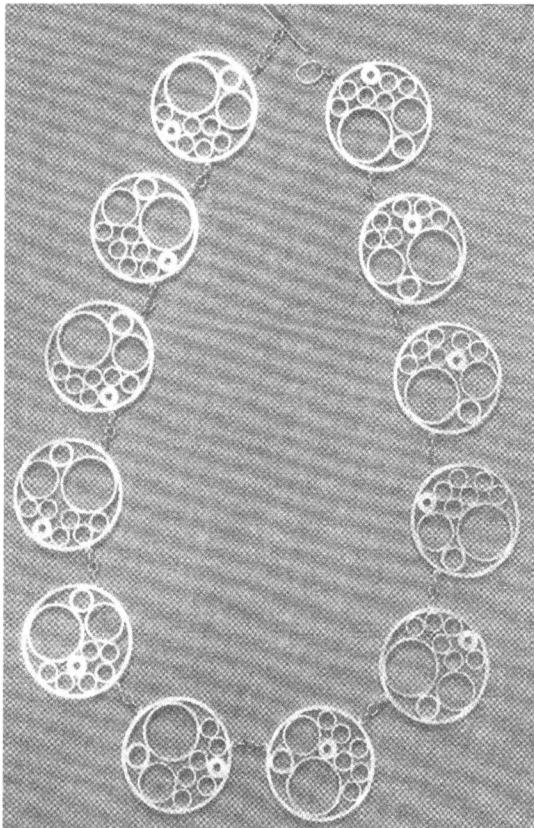

This is another example of constructing within a larger hollow section {see no. 9). The three larger hollow sections within the outside one are similarly positioned in all the units of the necklace. They were subsequently turned upside down. The seven smaller units are repeated in the compound units, but are in different positions in each one. This is clearly seen from the round, thick-walled, hollow section.

Note The 'ears' of round hollow sections used for joining the necklace units to each other are possibly too fine. The weight of the compound necklace units may cause the links to wear away the thin walls of these small sections. In this event, a major repairing job would have to be done, replacing them with larger hollow sections.

Plate 11:
Two related pendants
Photo: Photo Studios Ltd

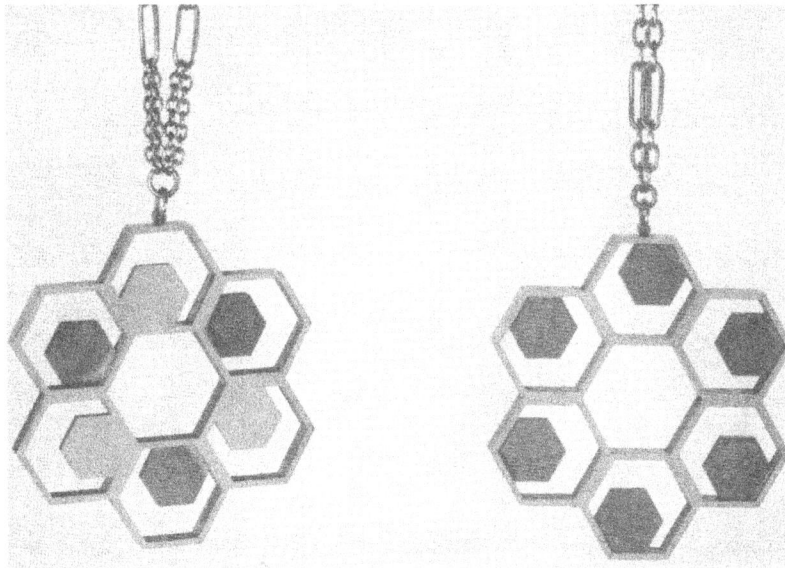

Size: Maximum width across each pendant - 1⅞"
Material: standard silver
Main units: hexagonal hollow sections, hexagonal solid rod sections

These two pendants show two possible ways among many of using hexagonal rods and hollow sections in combination. In the first pendant, the compound unit was made by placing the rod in a corner of the hollow section, flush with the surface of one side (fig 107).

FIG 107

There are six of these compound units, and they have been assembled in a rotational order with the rod sections nearest to the centre of the pendant. An additional variation was also introduced. On each of the sides of the pendant, alternate compound units were positioned so that the rod sections were flush with the surface.

The compound units of the second pendant are almost the same, except that the rod sections are not flush with either surface but are positioned approximately halfway through the hollow sections. These six compound units have also been assembled in a rotational order, but here the rod sections are nearest to the outside of the pendant. The 'ear' for the joining link on both pendants is a small, round, hollow section. The pendants have been blackened and then both surfaces highly polished.

Plate 12:
Pendant and Chain
Photo: Photo Studios Ltd

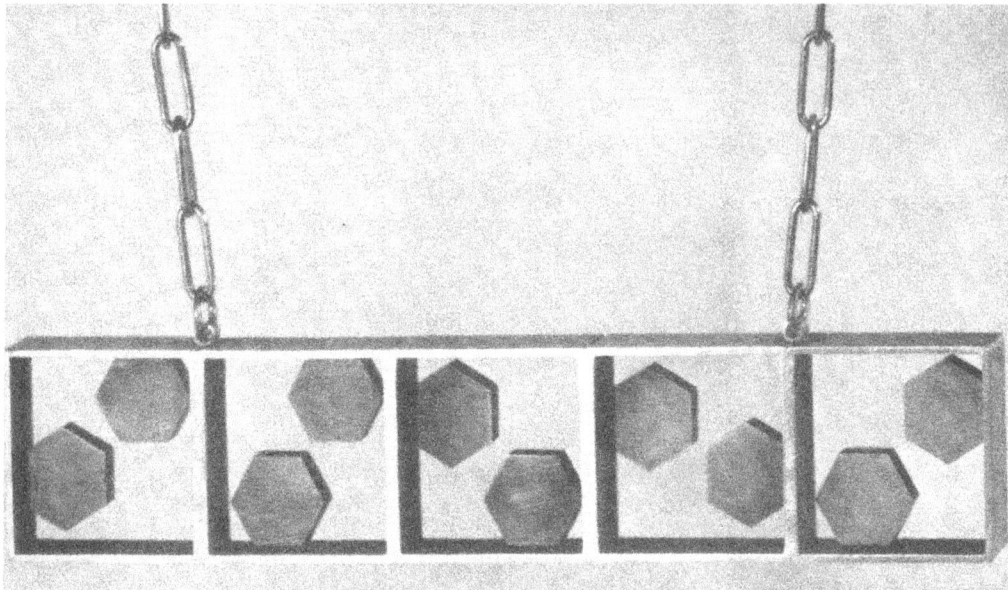

Size: 4$\frac{1}{2}$ x $\frac{7}{8}$"
Material: Standard silver
Main units: square hollow sections, sections of hexagonal rod, chain links modified to oblong
Shapes

It is possible to combine units which have many different attributes because of one or two primary common factors. In this case, the most usable common factor is that the straight edges of the hexagons are rectangular surfaces, as are the inside and outside faces of the square sections. The hexagon edges are small enough to fit inside the square and to be placed in a few determined positions along the larger rectangle. The hexagonal rod sections were placed about three-quarters along the width of the square section, which means that they are not flush with either side of the pendant but are clearly articulated units.

The chain is made of repeated units. Because of the many differing qualities of the hexagonal and square sections, it would probably have been a mistake to make a chain of more than one unit. Note the positions of the small, joining, hollow sections. Placing them halfway along any of the squares would have had the effect of 'cutting' the squares in half. Placing them on the extreme edges of the pendant would have minimized the effect of the long rectangular shape. This is because wh011 two ends of a chain are joined to a specific shape, they can, if badly placed, act as lines which extend the shape - even changing it altogether.

Plate 13:
Pendant and chain
Photo: Photo Studios Ltd

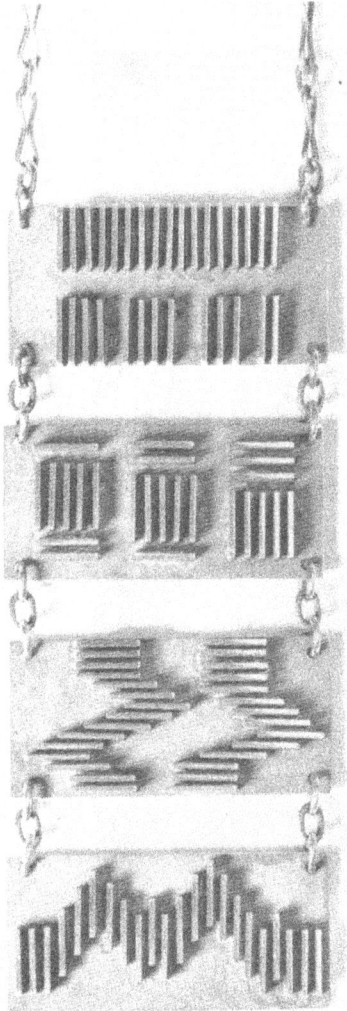

Size: 3³/₄" x 1¹/₂"
Material: fine silver
Main units: large and small rectangles

The soldering of many units like these on to a large surface presents some difficulties. It can and perhaps should be done in one soldering operation.

First the edge surfaces of the small units must be flat, otherwise they will not stand upright. Second, and most important, is to have the probe constantly hovering to adjust any unit which might lean over to one side. Occasionally these units, if placed close together, slide towards each other and become soldered. In this case, it will be necessary to remove both units and replace them. The secret in this kind of soldering is to 'freeze' the action at the exact moment when all possible adjustments with the probe have been achieved while the solder is in flow. At the appropriate moment, the flame must be quickly and suddenly reduced to nothing.

These four compound units were originally assembled close together, being joined by two single links. It was interesting to discover that even though all the smaller units are similar and are all soldered on to similar larger units, the four compound units did not look well so close together. This may be because the small units were arranged within each rectangle quite independently of the other compound units, giving each one a self-contained quality. Using extra links allows spaces between them which act as individual frames. This frame effect confirms the self-contained quality of each compound unit, while placing them close together destroyed it. Despite similarities between these compound units, it is still not clear that they go well together. There is perhaps too much difference between the arrangements within each compound unit, and it may be that even more inter-relationship is necessary than the existing similarities.

The larger chain units are oblong modifications of round links, joined by smaller oblong links.

Plate 14
Necklace
Photo: Tony Stone

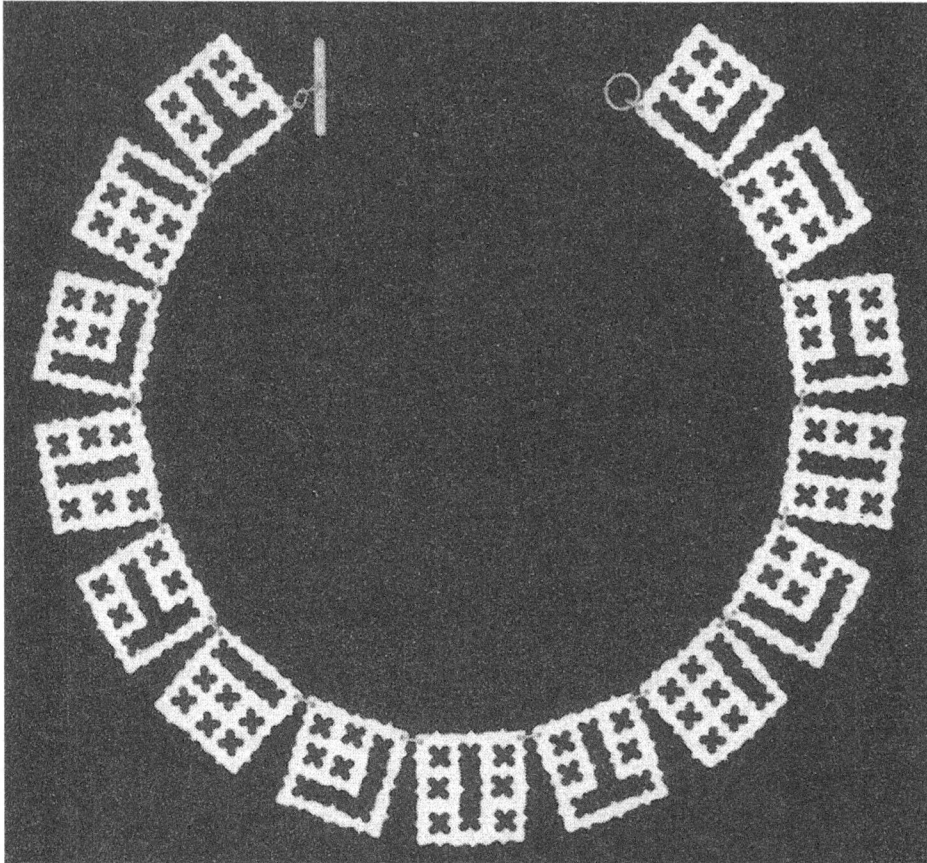

Size: units are approximately 1" square
Material: standard silver
Main units: cutouts from grid no. 2

These similar square pieces shape cut from grid no. 2 have been modified by cutting from within. There are three internal variations plus a 'spacer'. The variations are a T shape, an L shape, and an I shape placed at one side of the square. The shapes can change their positions four times without recurring. The central I shape is repeated three times as a 'spacer' between the groups of three, and has only been added to make up the length of the necklace. The necklace was subsequently gold-plated.

Plate 15
Necklace
Photo: Photo Studios Ltd

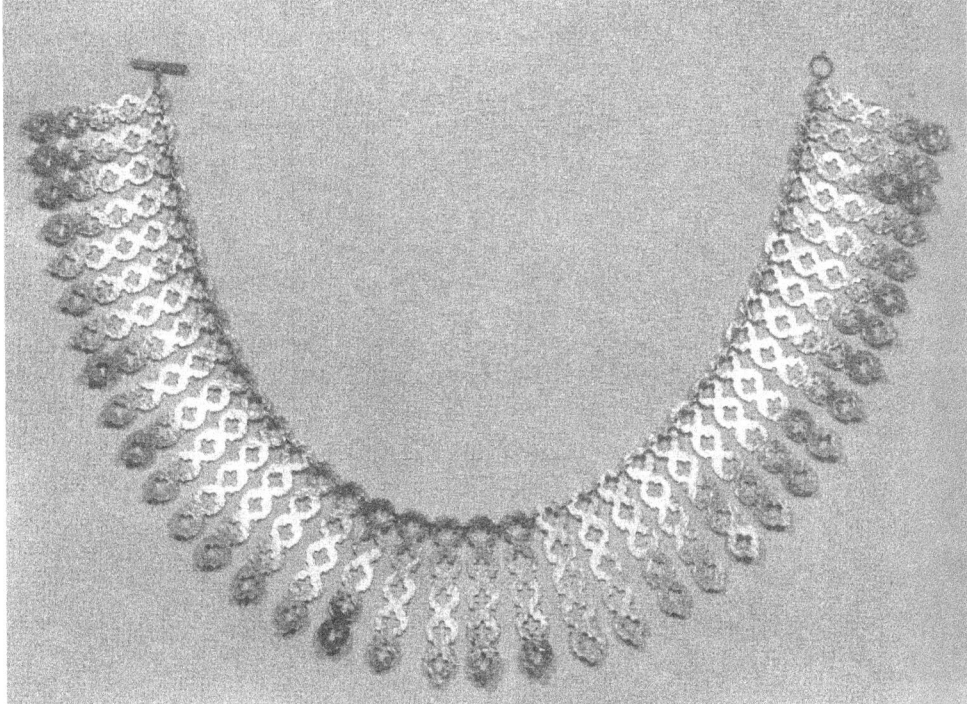

Size: length of unit - approximately 2"
Material: standard silver
Main units: units cut from grid no. 2, small joining links soldered and modified to an oblong shape

After cutting out these units from the grid, they were smoothed round the edges by first filing, taking care not to file away any of the essential parts of the grid. A small scotch stone was then used, and after that a burnisher. The units were then smoothed on both sides with two or three grades of emery paper placed on the steel block. Then they were textured with the ball head of the chasing hammer, giving the units a slight curve upwards. There were two reasons in this case for the texturing: to strengthen the units, and to unify the surface because of slight irregularities in the original perforating process. The necklace was subsequently gold plated.

Changing the appearance of materials

In art one has to think a great deal about changing the appearance of the materials one uses, for an artist may well ask himself: why work in one material and yet in the finish change its appearance so that it looks like another. For example, working in steel provides a reason for totally covering all the surfaces, because steel corrodes and must be protected. But when there is a serious doubt about falsifying the appearance of the material, one may have to decide not to use steel at all. This question arises a great deal in jewelry, where plating is common practice. One may wish to plate copper and brass because the tarnish which so easily develops marks the clothing. Or, if copper and brass are used in one piece of work, one may wish to unify the colour by plating it silver or gold. Another possibility is that one makes a piece in silver and considers that the particular construction needs to remain bright in order for its structure to be properly recognized. Gold-plating the work will ensure a much longer period of brightness. And so the question then becomes: does a clear view of the work supersede in importance the actuality of its making, for the reality of its structure remains, whether or not it is easily perceived. Many artists past and present have changed the appearance of the materials they used in one way or another, and the philosophic answer to this question is not an easy one to arrive at. Nevertheless, it is an important question to consider.

Plate 16:
Pendant and chain
Photo: Photo Studios Ltd

Size: 6^{1}/$_{4}$" x 2^{1}/$_{2}$"
Material: Standard silver
Main units: 7 similar units cut from grid no. 2

Continual exploration of these grids is the only way to uncover the more complex patterns contained within them, and therefore one must return to them again and again. Having cut the outside and inside shapes, the decision was made to join the units together in a vertical arrangement at three points. The holes were drilled and the units joined to each other by three links in three positions. When joining horizontal units to each other in this way in more than two positions, the distances between the joining holes must be absolutely accurate, otherwise the units will come to rest on two only of the joining links, causing both an imbalance and also a degree of rigidity. It was discovered after all the holes were drilled, that the units, when linked to each other, would not hang correctly. This was due not only to personal inaccuracies, but also to slight irregularities in the grid.

Handling the accidental

Mistakes are part of everyone's life, and by everyone I do of course include myself. The question arising from them is always the same one: how do we handle them?

Mistakes and accidents can be very instructive and can lead to many discoveries. And so when they occur to the work through an error in judgment or even a slip of the hand holding a tool, the first question should always be, 'Can I use it?' That is to say, can the result of the mistake, when it is properly analysed and assessed, be instructive in any way? Can it be used to modify and improve the piece by suggesting something which would not otherwise have been thought of? The answers to these questions are very often positive, and one should always keep the mind open to these possibilities.

The case now in question is the silver pendant. What was learned was that when several horizontal units are joined together in three or more positions, the distances between the joining holes must be precise. Also, that a slight inaccuracy with two joining links will not prevent similar units from hanging correctly. This is not to say that the link holes should not in any case be so accurate. This particular mistake could have been covered over by either soldering or by riveting a piece of round wire of the same diameter into the holes. Since the units had already been textured and therefore hardened, any soldering would have negated this process. Therefore the latter of the two possibilities was decided on, namely, to rivet in a piece of round wire.

Now why cover up one's mistakes? It may be useful sometimes to let them show in a modified form, if only to remind oneself of the occasion. And so it was decided to use 18 carat yellow gold wire. This shows the mistake and at the same time gives an added interest to the piece. The cut off sections of gold wire were hammered in like rivets.

The chain is compounded of large, round, handmade links and sections of machine-made silver chain.

Plate 17
Pendant and chain
Photo: Photo Studios Ltd

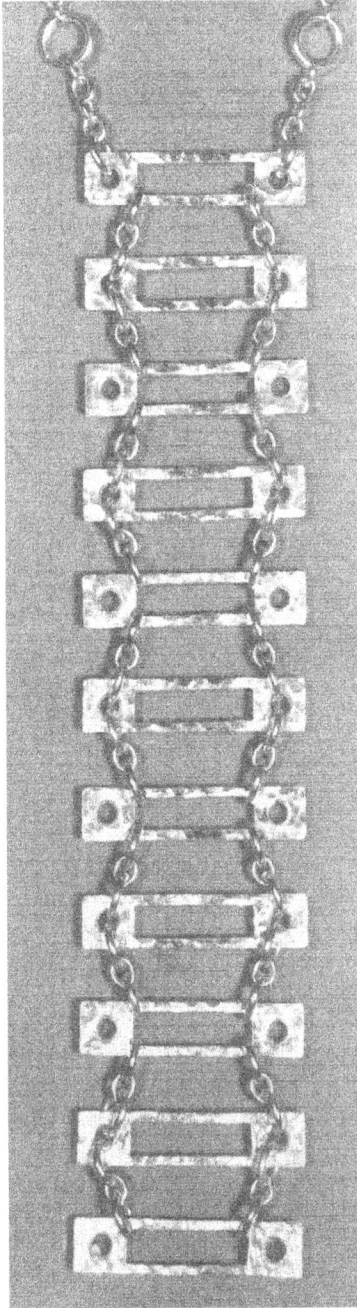

Size: 8" x 1³/₄"
Materials: brass and copper
Main units: striking plates, chain section, jump rings

The units called striking plates are usually screwed into door frames and receive the bolt of the lock which is fitted to the door. They have been annealed and then textured to soften their mechanical look. They are joined to each other by sections of machine-made copper chain and brass jump rings, which are linked through alternate round and rectangular openings, thus producing vertical zig-zag lines. The chain from which the pendant hangs is also composed of sections of machine-made chain and brass jump rings. The pendant has been gold-plated, thus unifying the colour (see notes for plate 15).

Plate 18
Necklace
Photo: Photo Studios Ltd

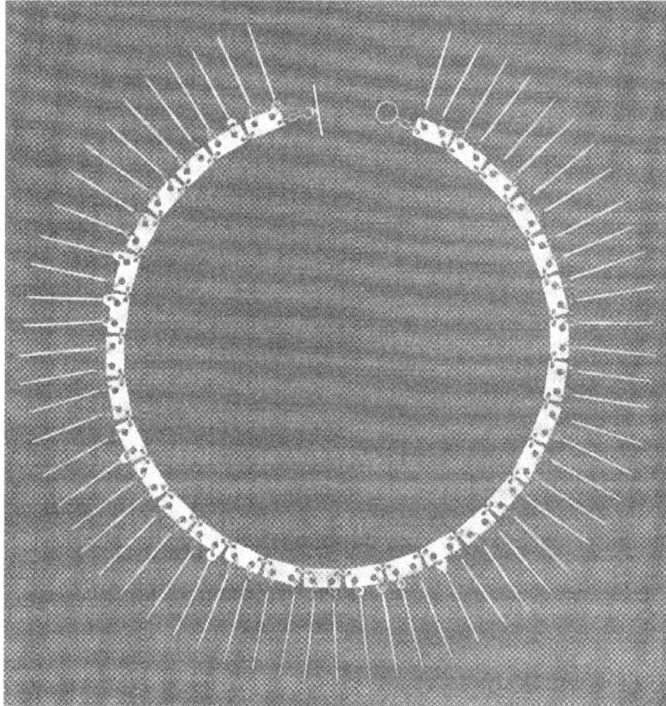

Size: length of vertical units - 1¼"
Material: fine silver
Main units: electrical contacts, silver posts (fig 108)

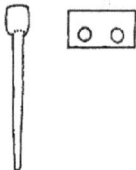

FIG 108

These silver posts are used in dentistry for root therapy. When the pulp has to be removed from the root canals of the tooth, these fine silver pieces, which are very slightly conic in shape, are inserted into the now hollow roots. This procedure lengthens the useful life of the tooth and helps to prevent it from crumbling. The ends are flattened in order for the dentist to hold the posts while pushing them in. They are subsequently nipped off with pliers. Silver posts can become useful units by drilling holes into the flattened ends. The rectangular units were stamped with the two larger holes. These holes were used to hang the silver posts, and so two further holes had to be drilled for joining them to each other. The joining links were soldered and then made oblong in shape.

Plate 19
Necklace
Photo: Tony Stone

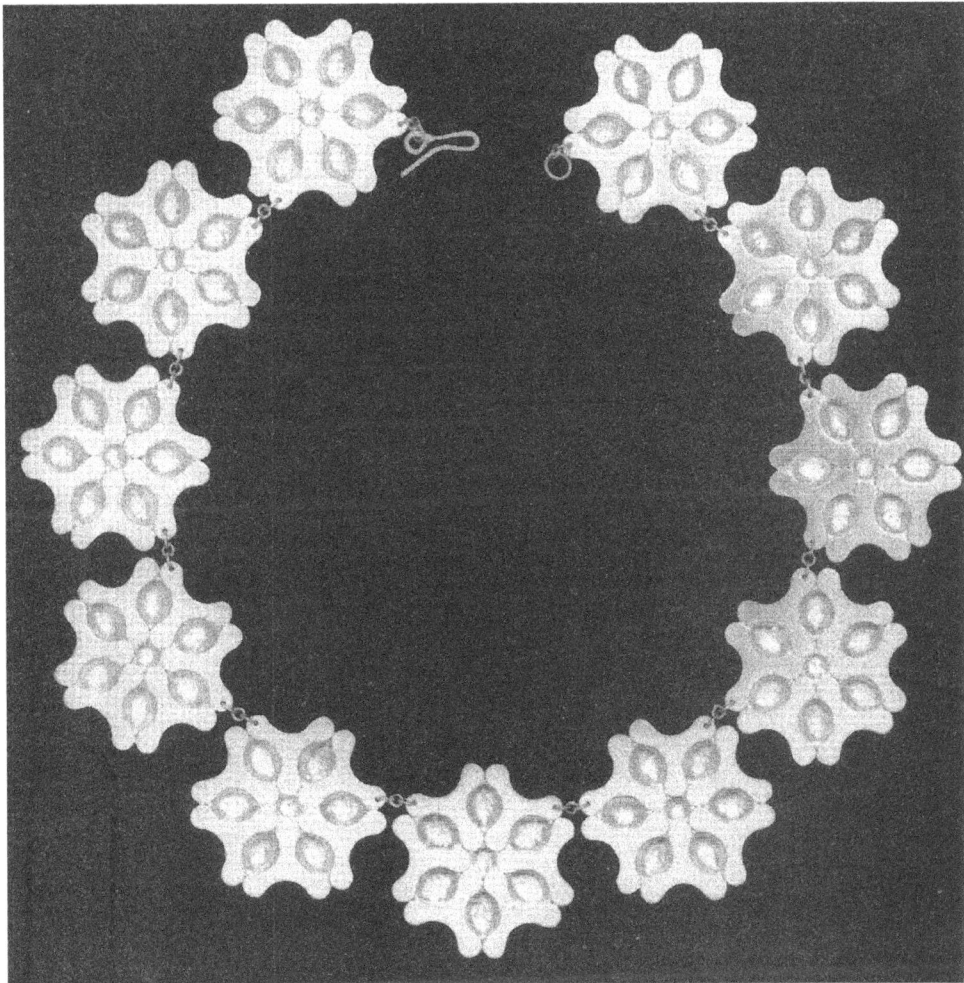

Size: maximum width of units, $1\frac{1}{2}$"
Material: standard silver
Main units: burrs from grid no. 4 soldered to round silver blanks

This necklace is made in the same way as the one shown in plate no. 20, except that here the forming units of each compound unit are six 'propeller' shaped burrs from grid no. 4. The joining links may be too fine for the size and bulk of the necklace units. These units would certainly not lose anything by having larger joining links. Also, there are at least two other possible positions for drilling the link holes.

Plate 20:
Necklace
Photo: Tony Stone

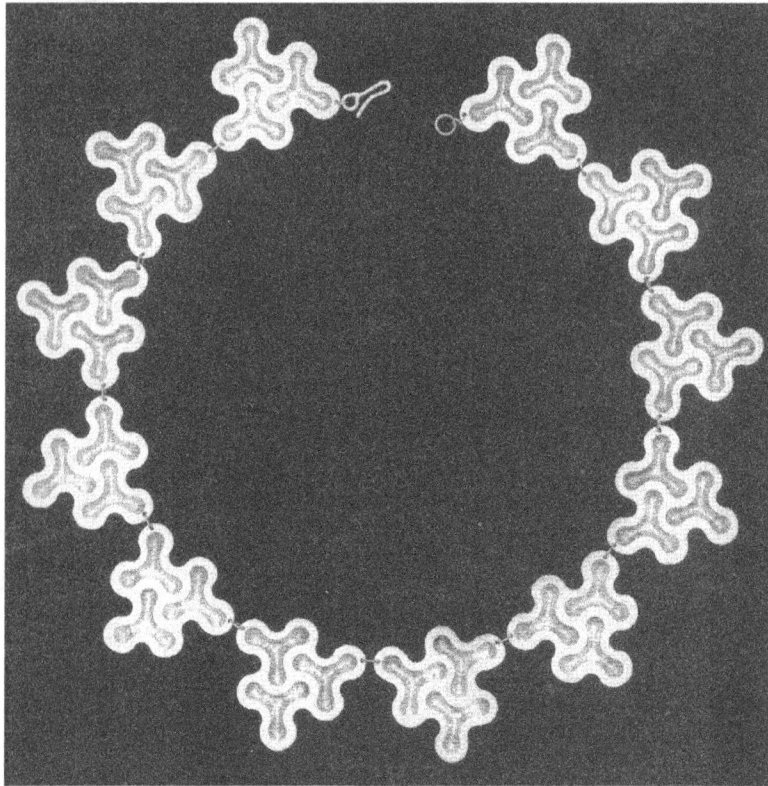

Size: maximum width of units, 1$\frac{1}{2}$"
Material: standard silver
Main units: cut out part from grid no. 4, soldered on to thin silver blanks

These repeated units have been arranged in mirror opposition to each other, and the consequent difference between them is quite interesting. Also note the differences of the spaces between the compound units and how these units look slightly different as their positions change round the circle.

After this shape was cut from the grid, it was soldered to a fine gauge silver blank. The whole piece was set in wax and then the 'propeller' shapes were recessed by means of the doming punch. This process is known as repoussé, and is usually done by setting the piece into pitch, which is very much harder than wax (see Tools and Processes). After this operation, the round blank was cut with a fine saw to the same outside shape as the grid piece. Holes were then drilled for joining the compound units.

Plate 21
Pendant and chain
Photo: Photo Studios Ltd

Size: length – 3$\frac{1}{2}$"
Material: standard and fine silver
Main units: grid no. 1, silver rivets

The seven star shapes contained within the 'cross' shape were cut first. This grid, as previously stated, is based on angles of 60° and 120°, and in order to achieve the pattern of the cross, many holes had to be left intact. The holes surrounding the seven star shapes have been filled with flat-headed rivets.

Next, a surrounding line of star shapes were cut, inserting rivets into untouched holes. The outside shape was decided and cut accordingly. The whole piece was then repeated, and the two completed sides riveted together. Four holes on each piece were left open for this purpose: top, bottom and both sides. Since the two sides of the pendant are identical, it was decided not to use the same flat-headed rivets for riveting them together, for the flat heads would then show on one side only, thus breaking the similar structure of the two sides. It was decided to use round wire to do the riveting job. It so happened that wire of the right gauge to fit the holes was not available at that time. One must improvise in such circumstances, and so short lengths of round, hollow sections of the right diameter, with wire inserted into them, were used as rivets.

An extra hole at the top was left open for attaching a link. To give this double-sided hole the same quality as the rest of the pendant, a short length of round, hollow section was riveted into this hole, and the first link passes through it. The chain is composed of three-hole cutouts of grid no. 1, and large links.

Note Use a pointed punch and chasing hammer to rivet the round, hollow sections. The conic shaped point of the punch spreads the sides of the hollow sections, thus preventing them from slipping out (fig 109).

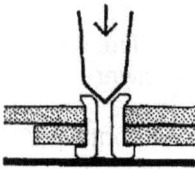

FIG 109

This is done at both ends, and then the riveting action is completed either with a flat punch and chasing hammer or with the ball head of this hammer.

Plate 22
Necklace
Photo: Photo Studios Ltd.

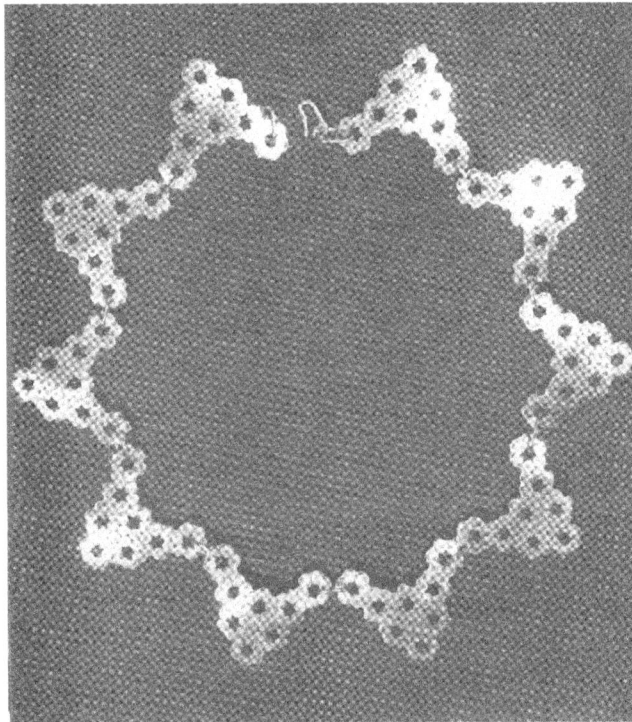

Size: maximum width across necklace unit, 1¹/₄"
Materials: fine and standard silver
Main units rivets, grid no. 1

Grid no. 1 has been modified as shown on page 37, the outside shape being different as the whole unit is composed of nine star shapes instead of only three.

Despite having cut into the holes of the grid, the holes are still three-quarters complete, and it is possible to fix rivets into them so that they cannot subsequently move if the shanks fit tightly into the holes. The rivets are fixed in the usual way. Note that the centre of each compound unit is solid. This means that the star shape has not been cut out at this point: the complete holes in the grid have been left intact.

The compound necklace units have been joined together through their existing holes by a heavy gauge wire link which was soldered and then made oblong. In this case, making the link oblong increases the distance between the necklace units without having to use a larger diameter link.

Plate 23
Necklace
Photo: Photo Studios Ltd

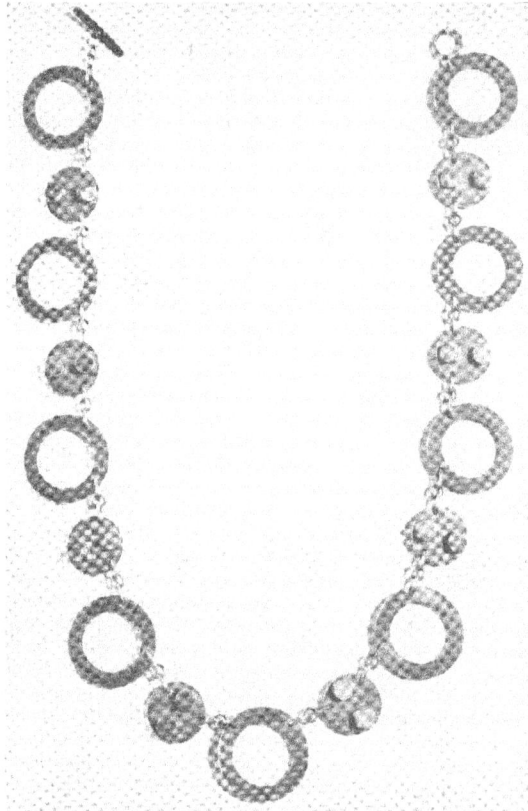

Size: outside diameter of washer shapes, $^{15}/_{16}$"
Material: fine silver
Main units: stampings

The large round blank is the same diameter as the inside diameter of the washer shape. It happens that they are not of the same gauge, which means that the one did not come from the other. However, this particular necklace is worth noting, as it shows one way to relate burrs to the grids from which they come.

The two, small, round blanks give added interest to the two main necklace units. Note their heavy gauge. Strong shear marks were visible on the sides caused by the punching out process. These marks had to be filed away with a needle file, and then the sides were stoned and finally smoothed with polishing emery paper. The necklace was blackened, and afterwards the top surfaces of the protruding round blanks were highly polished, as well as the edges of the two main units.

Plate 24
Necklace
Photo: Photo Studios Ltd

Size: diameter of blank, $^5/_8$"
Materials: fine silver; links, standard silver
Main units: round blanks, stampings

The tripodal stamping was riveted to the blank in the same position. However, it has also been alternately rotated into two different positions so that in one position one of its feet is at the bottom of the blank, and in its second position one of the spaces between the feet takes the bottom position of the blank.

The stamping was first textured in order to give it a different surface quality from the round blank, and then a hole was drilled in its centre corresponding to the shank of a round-headed rivet. The stamping was then placed in position so that the bottom hole on the round blank could be accurately determined and then drilled. The stamping is then fixed to the round blank by the rivet. The compound units are joined by a large, heavy gauge link. This was decided because of the heavy gauge of the round blank and stamping. It also adds depth to the necklace. The polishing of the top surfaces was done by hand with a piece of chamois leather.

Plate 25
Chain necklace
Photo: Tony Stone

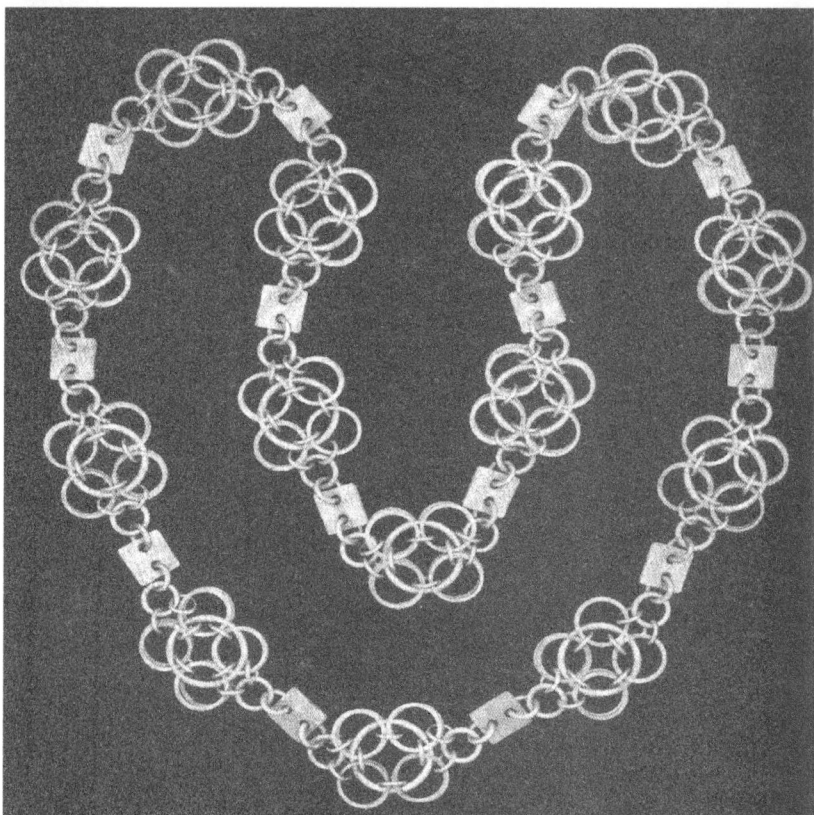

Size: outside diameter of large central link, ¾"
Materials: copper and brass
Main units: square blanks, four different sized links, thin brass washers

This relatively complex chain was constructed towards the end of a continuous exploratory period of chain making. It should be noted that in every kind of exploratory work, complexity is arrived at only by proceeding step by step. One cannot, having never made a chain, begin by making this particular chain, for the imagination of what is possible is always based on what is already known or on what has already been done. The so-called great leaps of the imagination are perhaps not so great as we like to believe. They are the sum of a series of small steps - each one based on and dependent upon the other. Of course, once any complexity has been arrived at, it is possible for anyone with related experience to copy and so repeat it without the work and discovery which precedes it. But this is not exploration.
All the links are open, and the square blanks are actually burrs from a square grid.

Plate 26
Pendant and chain
Photo: Tony Stone

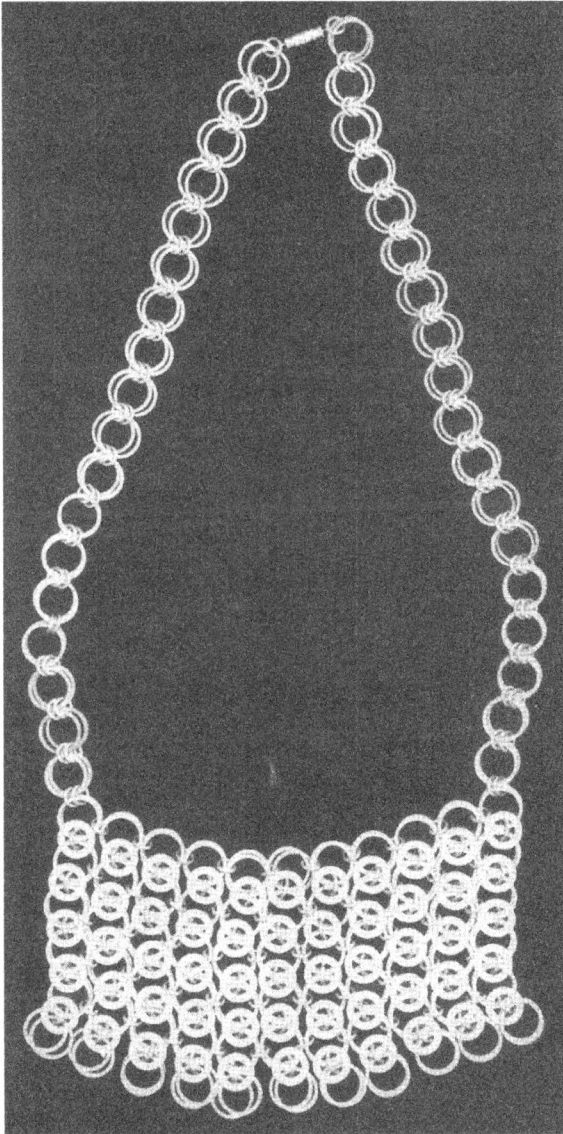

Size: 5$\frac{1}{2}$" x 3$\frac{1}{4}$"
Materials: brass and copper
Main units: brass washers and copper links

This pendant concluded the period of chain making mentioned in the notes for plate no. 25. It also has the kind of complexity which is gradually arrived at by working with similar units over and over again. The size of the pendant was arbitrarily chosen. It could in fact have been wider and longer. The effect of this pendant is like that of chain-mail, except that the pendant is rather more rigid.

Plate 27
Chain necklace
Photo: Photo Studios Ltd

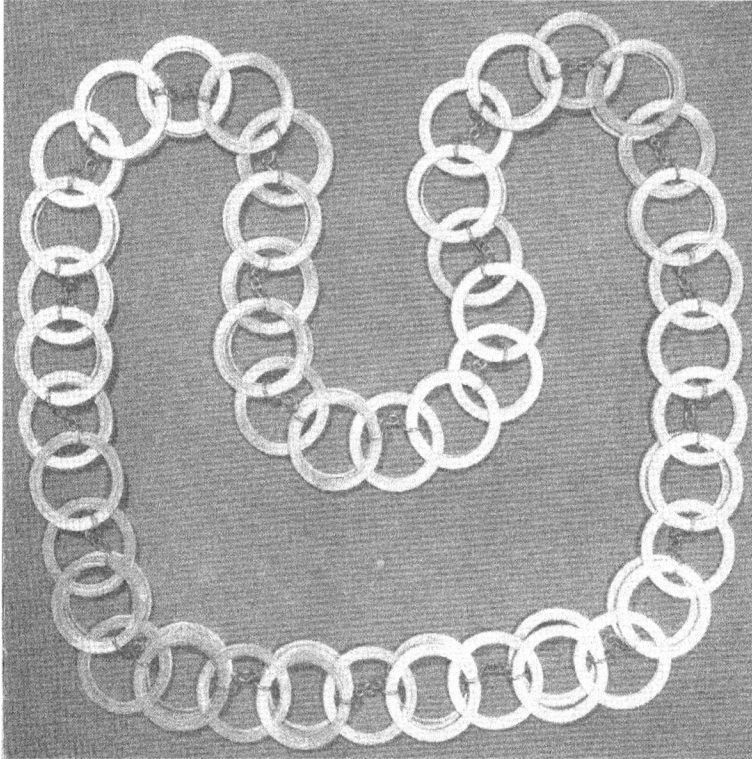

Size: outside diameter of round units, 1"
Materials: brass and copper
Main units: curtain rings

These hollow, brass, curtain rings have been flattened by placing them on a steel block and hammering with the flat head of the ball-pein hammer. The rings are all assembled in pairs, though this is not obvious in the photograph. Alternate pairs are separated by pushing an intermediate pair between them. The intermediate pairs are caught in position by the short chain length which connects the separated pairs of rings. The links are brass jump rings, and the short chain length is machine-made copper chain. The movement of this chain is rather like that of a bicycle chain. This is to say, it moves much more easily in one plane than any other.
Note: These hollow curtain rings should never be placed in acid, because the join in them is not soldered and therefore not properly sealed. This means that the acid seeps into them and cannot be removed. When this happens, the curtain rings will gradually disintegrate. The flattening process, if it is thoroughly accomplished, will allow the rings to be placed in the acid.

Plate 28
Eight chain portions
Photo: Photo Studios Ltd

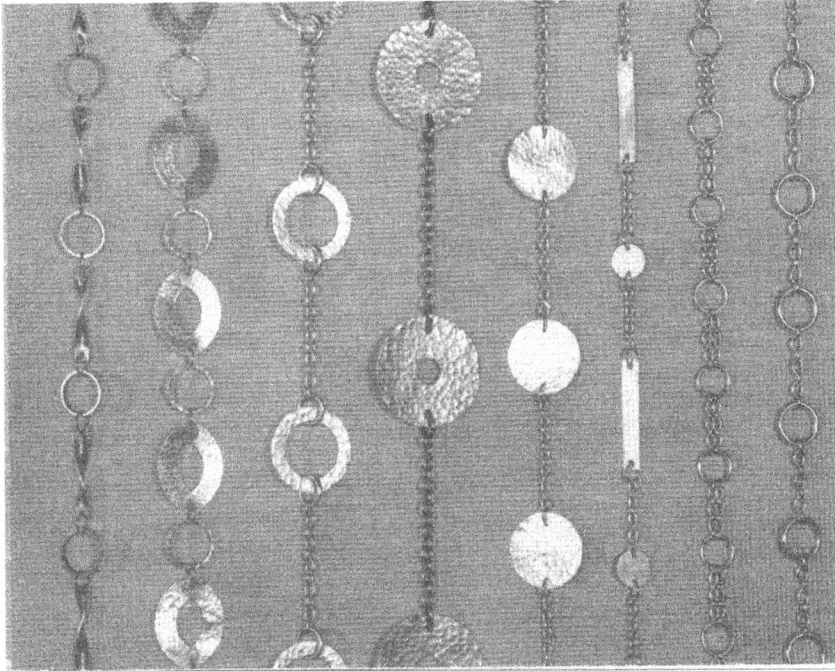

Size: full length of chains, 30"- 32"
Diameter of large washer in chain D, 1½"
Materials silver - standard and fine; copper and brass
Main units: hollow sections, stampings, blanks, burrs, machine-made chain sections and washers

Chain A: (reading from left to right): round hollow sections are joined to fine silver rectangular stampings by one link. The rectangles were stamped with a hole at one end. Another hole was drilled and the unit was twisted once. All the links are soldered and the chain was blackened and then polished.

Chain B: fine silver stampings (fig 110) of a thin gauge were hardened by texturing. They were joined by a single link to two very thin and textured round hollow sections. All the links were soldered and the chain blackened and polished.

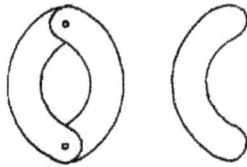

FIG 110

Chain C: brass washers were annealed and textured. The texture in this case was used to soften the hard mechanical look of the washer, a quality which is very dominant in large scale blanks and stampings in non-precious metals. The washers are joined by link to sections of machine-made chain. The links are open and the chain has been gold plated.

Chain D: large brass washers were textured for the same reason as for chain C. Extra holes were drilled for joining the washers to the machine-made chain by links. These links are, in this case, jump rings, which can be bought and were left unsoldered. This chain has also been gold-plated.

Chain E: fine gauge copper blanks were strengthened by texturing. The blanks were then joined to sections of machine-made chain by jump rings left unsoldered. The chain was then gold-plated.

Chain F: rectangular copper burrs from grid no. 3 were joined by links and machine-made chain to round copper blanks. The links were left unsoldered and the chain was gold-plated.

Chains G and H: round links - jump rings - in brass were joined to sections of machine-made chain and left unsoldered. Chain G has double chain sections between jump rings. Both chains were gold-plated.

Plate 29
Earrings
Photo: Photo Studios Ltd

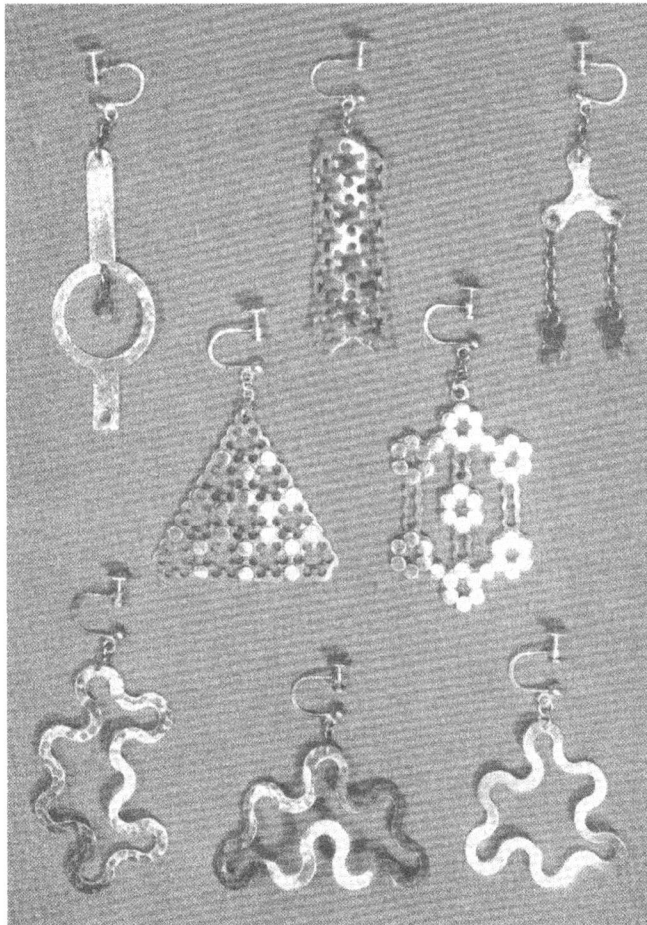

Size: length of earring A, 2 $\frac{3}{16}$"
Materials: fine and standard silver
Main units: electrical contacts, grid nos. 1 and 4, burr from grid no. 4

Earring A is made from an electrical contact stamping. Its only modifications are hardening by texturing, and insertion of a silver rivet at the bottom to give the piece extra weight and also to act as a visual 'stop'. Judged by eye, there is no reason why the 'foot' should be the length it is, and the rivet stops the eye from expecting to see more of it. The little chain with a coral bead hanging in the centre of the circle is only an embellishment and is not really necessary. There seems no reason why one should not occasionally embellish, so long as it never becomes an end in itself.

Earring B is a modification of grid no. 1. The strip has been placed on a round rod which is held in the bench vice. The piece is then hammered to take up the shape. The hammering has also caused a slight lifting at either end, giving the whole piece a saddle shape. The earring was then polished.

Earring C is made with one burr from grid no. 4. The chains are machine-made, with small round blanks at the ends to which are attached blue china beads. Again the bends are an embellishment, but the chain and blanks accent one direction of an otherwise three-directional unit. These earrings were textured, blackened and lightly polished.

Earrings D and E are modified pieces of grid no. 1, with rivets added to them. They were blackened and then the flat rivet heads highly polished.

Earrings F, G and H are modified pieces of grid no. 4. F and G have been hardened, shaped and textured with the hammer. Earring H has been hardened by twisting the three points in one direction. This modifies the otherwise flat unit and gives it a propeller-like quality.

Note: A pair of earrings need not necessarily consist of two identical earrings. A to E and G in the photograph are identical to the second in the pair, but F is in mirror opposition to its second, while H is not only in mirror opposition but has the three points twisted in the opposite direction. Perhaps the difference between earrings in a pair should only be a matter of two possible variations rather than a total difference of construction.

Plate 30
'Rectangular Bar Construction'
(1963)
Photo: Tony Stone

Size: height, 2"
Material: fine silver
Main units: rectangular bars

The system in this work follows one main rule: the units are arranged so that in plan the hole down the middle is never smaller than a square, and the units either sit on the edge of this square or at the outside edge of the construction. There are many variations even within this rigid system.
The piece has been brightened with a fine brass wire brush.

Plate 31
'Hexagonal Construction No.3'
(1965)
In the collection of: Mr & Mrs Alvan Macauley
Photo: Photo Studios Ltd

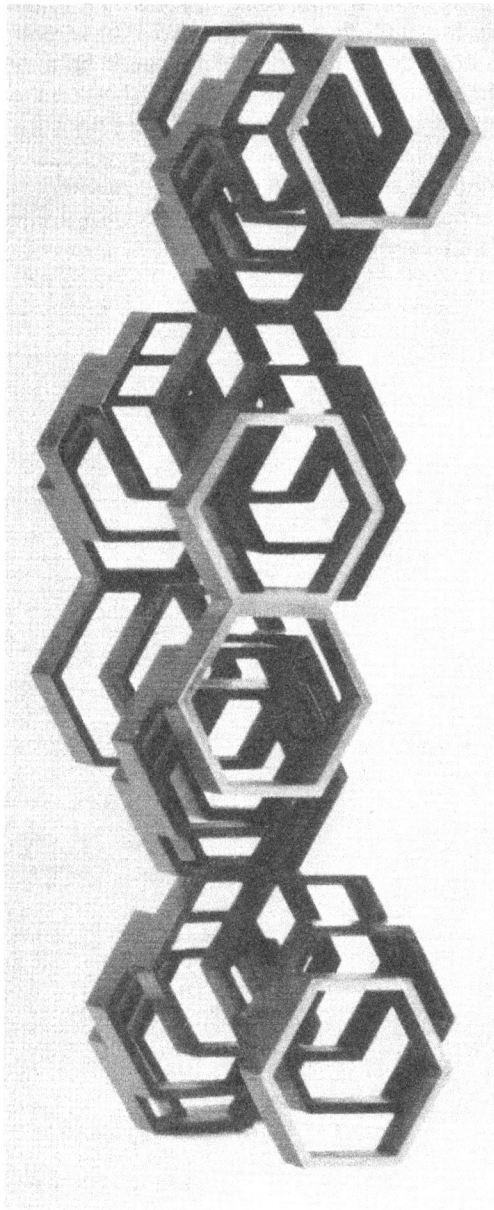

Size: height, 4"
Material: standard silver
Main units: hexagonal hollow sections

This construction is composed of four compound units of seven. That is to say, there are twenty-eight hexagonal hollow sections. The compound units are constructed in the same way, but are joined together at varying points. The construction has been blackened, and the first and seventh units in each compound unit have been highly polished.

Plate 32
'Octagonal Construction at the First Position' (1964)
Photo: Photo Studios Ltd

Size: length, 6"
Material: standard silver
Main units: octagonal hollow sections

These octagonal sections have been cut so that each of the flat facets is a square. This means that they can be precisely fitted together at these surfaces.
Starting with compound units of two hollow sections soldered together, these were assembled in a stepped spiral. A metal clip glued into the Perspex (Plexiglas) base allows one of the sides of an octagonal unit to slip underneath it and so to be held in position.

Plate 33
'Square Dislocation' (1965)
In the collection of Joseph H. Hirshhorn
Photo: Anthony Bregman

Size: approximately 4 ¼" in length
Material: standard silver
Main units: square hollow sections

This construction was built up vertically. Each unit is joined to the next by its cut face, and is stepped out one third of the length of a side. The four sets of spirals commence in the same position each time, but the position of the second unit in each spiral is rotated 90° to the preceding one, that is, four times in all. The last unit is an addition used as a stop. It begins a fifth spiral which would be a repeat of the first.

Plate 34
'Three-Unit Construction No. 1' (1963)
In the collection of Joseph H. Hirshhorn
Photo: Anthony Bregman

Size: approximately 4³/₄" in length
Material: standard silver
Main units: round hollow sections

This construction was built up vertically. Each layer consists of a compound unit made of three round, hollow sections joined in a triangular shape. The compound units were then assembled in a spiral, using one of the three joints of each preceding compound unit as a pivoting point.

Plate 35
'Interlocking Column No. 2' (1964)
Photo: Photo Studios Ltd

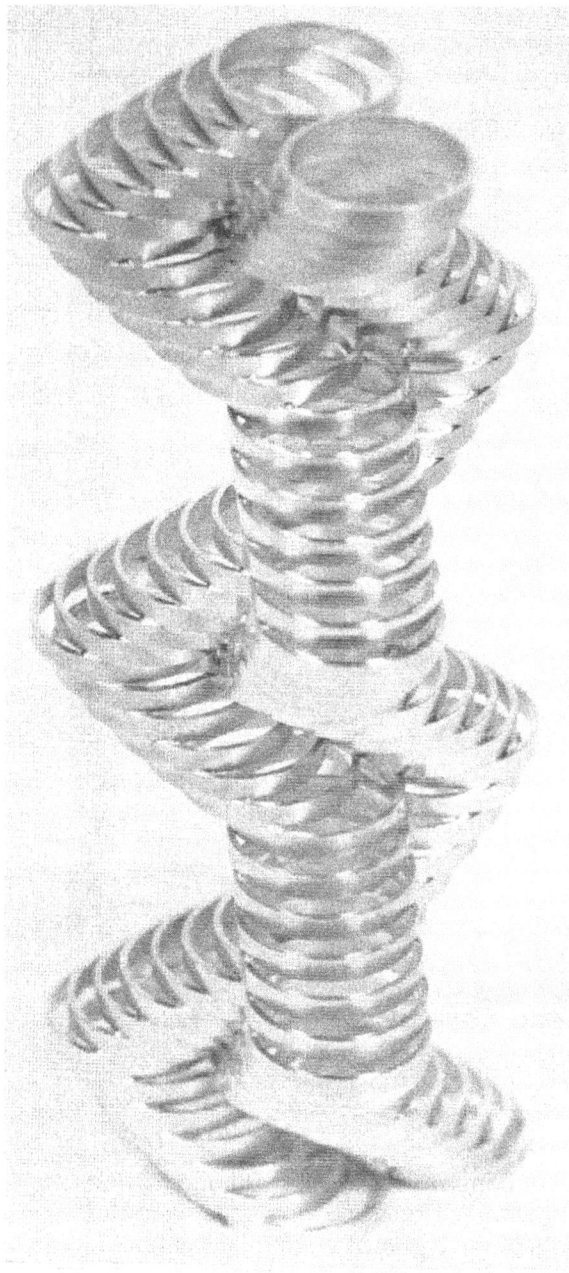

Size: height, 6"
Material: red and yellow 18 carat gold
Main units: round hollow sections

A series of compound units were made, each consisting of one yellow gold, round, hollow section and one red gold, round, hollow section, both of the same dimensions. The building up was carried out with these compound units. The construction spirals round in such a way that in plan it forms three 120 ° angles as shown in fig 111.

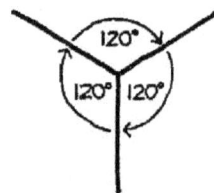

FIG 111

One column of the spiral is consistently yellow gold, while the second column is red gold. The two colours were chosen to emphasize the two-part nature of the compound units and therefore of the whole construction.

Plate 36
'Two-nodal Column' (1966)
Photo: Photo Studios Ltd

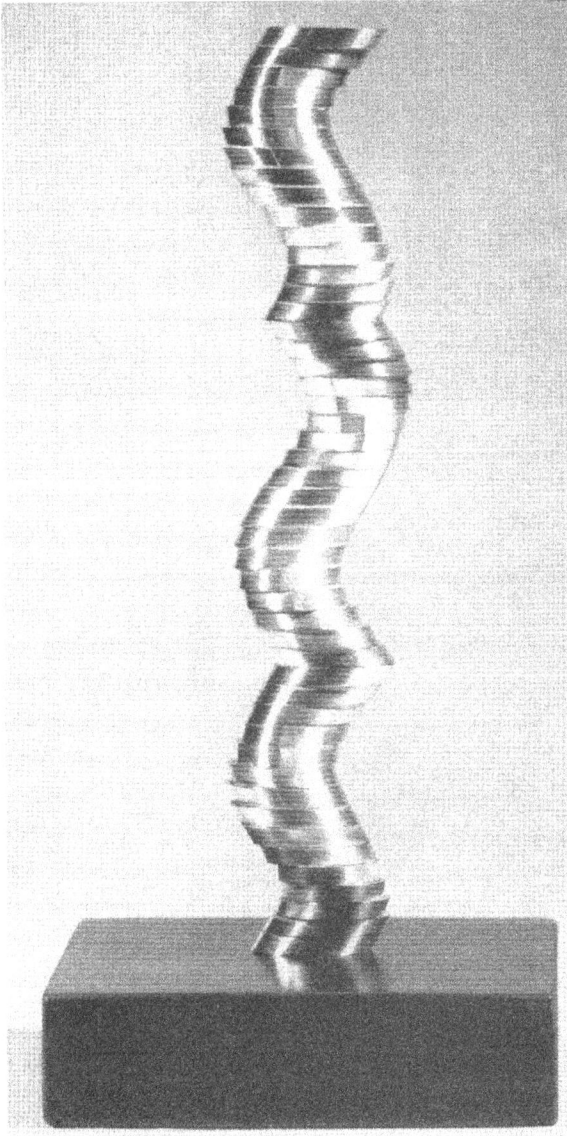

Size: 5 $\frac{1}{2}$" high
Material: standard silver
Main units: round hollow sections

These hollow sections have been cut off at a 60° angle in one plane. The units spiral round at a fixed point, and the nodes are introduced by reversing a unit at two positions. This creates the changes in the flow of the spiral.

Plate 37
'Flowering Spiral' (1964)
Photo: Photo Studios Ltd

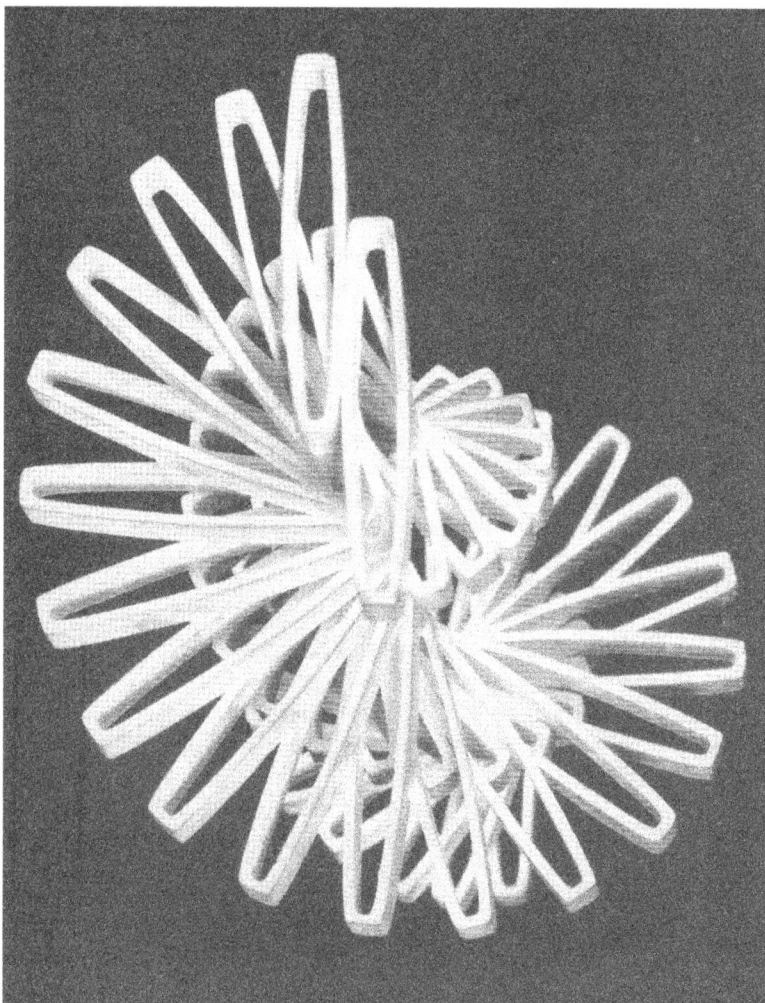

Size: height, 2"
Material: standard silver
Main units: oblong hollow sections

This is constructed with a series of compound units consisting of two similar single units soldered together. The building up began with the compound units pivoting about a vertical centre. The photograph has been taken from above.

Appendix

List of Suppliers

ENGLAND

The following suppliers have been used by the writer and have been found satisfactory

Johnson, Matthey & Company Limited
73-83 Hatton Garden, London EC1

This firm supplies the following: sheet, wire, hollow sections, solid rods, stampings, blanks and rivets. All these things are available in silver and some in gold. Hollow sections and solid rods can be cut into regular pieces by this firm. Round hollow sections in sizes up to ¼" outside diameter are kept in stock but other sizes and other shapes must be ordered. The special stampings referred to in chapter 4 are not easily available and perseverance is necessary to extract them. This is because they are made for industry in large numbers and special arrangements are needed to make left-over stampings available to individual craftsmen. The other problem is that the designs of some of the silver stampings belong to manufacturers, who may not wish them to be used by others. However, certain other blanks, although not kept in stock, are easily ordered. These blanks are stamped out for cuff links, but of course can be used for anything. There are seven shapes: square, hexagon, octagon, circle, a broad and a long oval, and a rectangle with the four corners cut off. They are available in one size only.* Rivets are available from stock and are known particularly as electrical contacts.
Catalogues to ask for: *Products and Services for the Craftsman in Precious Metals*; *Electrical Contacts*; *Carat Gold Alloys for the Goldsmith and Jeweller*.
*(see Note under Handy and Harman, U.S- Suppliers.)

E. Gray and Son Limited
12, 14 & 16 Clerkenwell Road, London EC1

All standard jewelry tools are available here. Also available are jeweler's findings, silver wire and machine-made chain. Illustrated catalogue available.

Charles Cooper Limited
92-93 Hatton Garden, London EC1

All standard jewelry tools are available here, as well as jeweler's findings. Standard workbenches may also be ordered. Illustrated catalogue available.

Buck and Ryan Limited
101 Tottenham Court Road, London W1

General tool suppliers including some jewelers' tools. The Unimat lathe is available here and also silver steel rods for link making. Illustrated catalogue available.

Frank Romany Limited
52 Camden High Street, London NW1

This firm stocks supplies for ironmongers and wood-workers. Copper rivets and washers, brass striking plates, curtain rings and other interesting units are available here.
Note: Most ironmongers will stock many of these items.

J. Smith and Sons
42-45 St. John's Square, Clerkenwell, London EC1

Largest suppliers of non-ferrous metals in London. Hollow sections, solid rods, round blanks, washers, rivets and wire. Partially illustrated catalogue available. Metal perforation also available. They supply the round hole 60° and 120° pattern grid in copper and brass with six different hole sizes and in one gauge only.

British Machine Chain Limited
Elm Road, New Malden, Surrey
Silver machine-made chain in various sizes and patterns.
Illustrated sheet available.

R. G. Springall & Company
104-5 Saffron Hill, Hatton Garden, London EC1
Silver machine-made chain in many sizes and patterns.

English Chain Company
Chain House, Woodbridge Street, London EC1
Copper and brass plated machine-made chain in various sizes and patterns; brass jump rings.
Illustrated catalogue available.

G. A. Harvey & Company (London) Limited
Woolwich Road, London SE7

This is a very large firm in which metal perforation is only one activity. 4'x2' is a standard size perforated sheet, although any size can be produced. Sheets are not usually kept in stock and have to be specially ordered. This firm will perforate precious metal sheets of a smaller size than the standard. The precious metal sheet to be perforated must be supplied to the firm since it does not stock precious metals.
Note: When perforated copper sheets are ordered, a special request must be made for the burrs to be collected, other wise they will be treated as scrap in the usual way.
Naturally the silver burrs will be returned, as the silver belongs to the customer supplying it.
A stimulating illustrated catalogue of patterns is available.

F. P. Richards Limited
60 Poland Street, London W1

This firm does silver and gold plating.

W. Canning & Company Limited
77 St. John Street, London EC1

Potassium sulphide crystals and liquid for silver blackening are available here.

List of Suppliers

UNITED STATES

Note: The author has had no personal experience with any of the firms listed directly below. Contact has been made only through correspondence requesting information and catalogues, and obviously there are many more firms of importance and interest in the U.S.

Handy and Harman
850 3rd Avenue, New York, N.Y.

This firm supplies silver and gold in sheet and wire. It also produces hollow sections and will cut them to customers' requirements. Silver and gold stampings are available, but not silver rivets. However, this firm supplies material to other firms who make rivets and could probably supply information about them.

Catalogues to ask for: *Silver for the Craftsman; An Introduction to Carat Golds for Hand Craftsmen; Handy and Harman Carat Gold Shapes.*

This last short folder illustrates some exciting shapes for unit construction which are also available in sterling silver. Many of them are stamped with a protruding loop for attaching a link. These can easily be removed to give the pure shape.

Note: It is worth enquiring into the way in which these units are stamped out. For example, if they are stamped from strips of sheet metal, it may be possible to obtain the leftover grid which will resemble a perforated sheet.

Allcraft Tool and Supply Company Inc
15 West 45th Street, New York 36, N.Y.

This firm supplies tools, metals and findings for jewelry, silversmithing and enameling. It supplies silver in sheet, wire, round and square hollow sections, silver and copper blanks, machine-made chain and many other items too numerous to mention here. Their catalogue no. 65 is very stimulating and exciting and is an excellent example of how a catalogue should be compiled. The Unimat lathe is well illustrated and described, as well as a power-driven Scroll saw which may be very useful for cutting off units from hollow sections and solid rods.

The Evans Findings Company Inc
55 John Street, Providence, Rhode Island

This firm specializes in findings and settings and makes them in gold, silver, brass, steel, stainless steel and other metals. Judging from their catalogue, many of these findings are far too elaborate for unit construction, but there are a few interesting possibilities such as hollow rivets, spacers and washers.

METAL PERFORATION
The following names were supplied by The American Society for Metals, Metals Park, Ohio, as three large metal perforating firms in the United States. There are many others.

Chase Brass and Copper Company Inc
1940 Rodney, Waterbury, Connecticut

Harrington and King Perforating Company Inc
5653 Fillmore, Chicago, Illinois

Beckley Perforating Company
333 North Avenue, Garwood, New Jersey

The following addresses may also be of interest to American readers

SMELTERS AND REFINERS

Leach and Garner Co
608 Fifth Avenue, New York, N.Y.
Specialists in gold, silver, gold-filled materials and metal laminated combinations.

Refining Division of Engelhard Industries Inc
429 Delancey Street, Newark, N.J.

Standard Platinum Co
25 West 17th Street

BASE METALS

T. E. Conklin Brass & Copper Co Inc
113 Leonard Street, New York, N.Y.

M ETAL FOILS

C. R. Hill Co
35 West Grand River, Detroit 26, Michigan

Welsh Gold Stampers
241 Centre Street, New York, N.Y.

Riverside — Alloy Metal Division
H. K. Porter Co Inc
1021 Stuyvesant Avenue, Union, New Jersey
The widest range of speciality alloys including bronze, brass, nickel silver, Inconel, stainless steel, Monel, and nickel-clad copper.

Ordering sheet metal and wire

It is common practice to refer to the thickness of sheet metal and wire by stating the gauge numbers. However, the situation is confusing, as there are several different gauge standards and the gauge number in one standard will not necessarily be the same in another. It is therefore advisable to state the thickness required in decimals or fractions of an inch, although one may need to modify one's requirements to whatever standard sizes are available.

Decimal and metric equivalents of common fractions

Fractions of an inch	Decimals of an inch	Equivalent in millimetres	Fractions of an inch	Decimals of an inch	Equivalent in millimetres
1/64	·01562	·397	33/64	·51562	13·097
1/32	·03125	·794	17/32	·53125	13·494
3/64	·04687	1·191	35/64	·54687	13·891
1/16	·0625	1·588	9/16	·5625	14·288
5/64	·07812	1·984	37/64	·57812	14·684
3/32	·09375	2·381	19/32	·59375	15·081
7/64	·10937	2·778	39/64	·60937	15·478
1/8	·1250	3·175	5/8	·625	15·875
9/64	·14062	3·572	41/64	·64062	16·272
5/32	·15625	3·969	21/32	·65625	16·669
11/64	·17187	4·366	43/64	·67187	17·066
3/16	·1875	4·763	11/16	·6875	17·463
13/64	·20312	5·159	45/64	·70312	17·859
7/32	·21875	5·556	23/32	·71875	18·256
15/64	·23437	5·953	47/64	·73437	18·653
1/4	·2500	6·350	3/4	·75	19·050
17/64	·26562	6·747	49/64	·76562	19·447
9/32	·28125	7·144	25/32	·78125	19·844
19/64	·29687	7·541	51/64	·79687	20·241
5/16	·3125	7·938	13/16	·8125	20·638
21/64	·32812	8·334	53/64	·82812	21·034
11/32	·34375	8·731	27/32	·84375	21·431
23/64	·35937	9·128	55/64	·85937	21·828
3/8	·3750	9·525	7/8	·875	22·225
25/64	·39062	9·922	57/64	·89062	22·622
13/32	·40625	10·319	29/32	·90625	23·019
27/64	·42187	10·716	59/64	·92187	23·416
7/16	·4375	11-113	15/16	·9375	23·813
29/64	·45312	11·509	61/64	·95312	24·209
15/32	·46875	11·906	31/32	·96875	24·606
31/64	·48437	12·303	63/64	·98437	25·003
1/2	·5	12·700	1	1·000	25·400

Temperature conversion:

°F to °C Subtract 32, multiply by 5, and divide by 9
°C to °F Multiply by 9, divide by 5, and add 32

Silver standards in Britain and the United States

British standard silver and American sterling silver differ in the following way: the silver content of both metals is approximately ·925 - that is to say, 925 parts per 1,000. However, for British hall-marking, the minimum permissible silver content when assayed is ·925, which means that the silver in sheet, wire etc, is rolled and drawn to a slightly higher silver content to ensure this minimum quantity. In the United States, an article with the 'Sterling' stamp must assay at a minimum silver content of ·921, which means that a silver content of ·925 is an average and that a differential of up to and perhaps more than ·004 may exist between British standard silver and American sterling silver.

Britannia silver
The only other hall-marking quality of silver recognized in Britain is Britannia silver. This must assay at a silver content of not less than ·958 and is sometimes known as better nine or simply as fine silver. Most of the fine silver electrical contacts mentioned in this book have a higher silver content than Britannia silver and will qualify for the Britannia hall-mark provided they are not mixed with any standard silver.

Bibliography

PRACTICAL INFORMATION

The Design and Creation of Jewelry by Robert von Neumann.
Pitman & Sons, London, 1962; Chilton Company, Philadelphia.

This is a very good informative book describing many important techniques necessary for making almost any kind of jewelry.

Metal Art Crafts by John G. Miller.
D. Van Nostrand Company Inc, Princetown, New Jersey.

Good sections on tools, operations and processes in metalcraft.

Metals Handbook
published by The American Society for Metals.

The aim of this large volume is '. . . to provide the reader with practical information that will help him select and control processes for the heat treating, cleaning and finishing of ferrous and non-ferrous metals'. This is a very informative, technical and scientific volume with many expert contributors.

PICTORIAL

Modern Jewelry by Graham Hughes.
Studio Vista, London, 1964: Crown Publishers Inc, New York, 1964.

This book gives a broad view of jewelry from 1890 to 1964 with some excellent photographs. Note the work of Nahum Slutsky, who worked at the Bauhaus in Germany, and also the work of Alexander Calder, whose jewelry consists mainly of handmade units.

A Concise History of Modern Sculpture by Herbert Read
Thames and Hudson, London, 1964; Frederick Praeger, New York, 1964.

Note work by: Alexander Rodchenko — *Construction of Distances*, 1920, made with repeated units of wooden blocks; *Hanging Construction*, 1920, made of washer-shaped units in wood, cut out from one large wooden circle and then hung one inside the other. Naum Gabo — *Constructed Head No. 2*, 1916, built up of sheets of metal welded together. Antoine Pevsner—*Column*, 1952, constructed with lengths of bronze and brass wires. A very full view of this artist's constructions in metal wire can be seen in the book **Antoine Pevsner**, published by Editions du Griffon, Switzerland. Constantin Brancusi —- *Torso of a Young Man*, 1924, shows this artist close to the constructive method. The shape of the first unit of the base was used repeatedly in his bases and in a sculpture called *Endless Column*, 1918. This work can be seen in **Brancusi** by David Lewis, Alec Tiranti, London, 1957; George Wittenborn, New York, 1957. Although carved in wood rather than constructed, this sculpture clearly demonstrates the repeated unit idea. This book also shows his pre-occupation with articulated shapes and his building with carved blocks.

MAGAZINES

Studio International, April 1966: note 'Construction in 30 equal elements, 1938/9, by Max Bill and articles on Constructivism.

The Structurist, edited by Eli Bornstein, University of Saskatchewan, Saskatoon, Canada. Distributors: London - Alec Tiranti; New York — George Wittenborn and Company. No. 3, 1963: note article by Edward and Jane Abramson; interview with Structurist artist Charles Biedermann, part I ; Structurist reliefs by Charles Biedermann and others. No. 4, 1964: interview with Charles Biedermann, part II; article by JoanSaugrain; Structurist reliefs by Charles Biedermann, Joan Saugrain and others.

www.ingramcontent.com/pod-product-compliance
Lightning Source LLC
Chambersburg PA
CBHW081233090426
42738CB00016B/3292